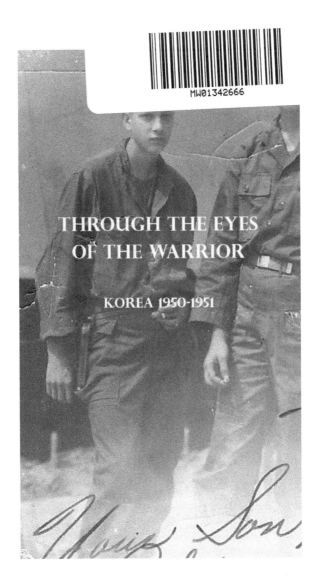

THROUGH THE EYES OF THE WARRIOR

KOREA 1950-1951

BY TIM SCHOONARD

"Pro Deo et Patria"

THROUGH THE EYES OF THE WARRIOR
Korea 1950-1951

The Combat Journey of
CORPORAL CHESTER THIESSEN

A 2nd U.S. Infantry Division
Soldier Remembers

TIM SCHOONARD

THROUGH THE EYES OF THE WARRIOR
KOREA 1950-1951

Copyright © 2013 by Tim Schoonard

Edited by: Monica L. Schoonard, M.A.

Cover Design by Tim Schoonard

Cover and Book Photos courtesy of Chester Thiessen
Chipyong-ni Battle map courtesy of General Paul Freeman, used with permission.
All other maps by author.
Author photo and purple heart photo courtesy of author.
Illustrative drawings contributed by Chester Thiessen, except,
Medal of Honor sketch (Chapter 15) which was compiled in honor of Chester Thiessen (1994) by an unnamed Fort Custer Military Training Center soldier.

ISBN: 978-1495272288

All Rights Reserved. This book may not be reproduced, transmitted, or stored in whole or in part by any means, including graphic, electronic, or mechanical without the express written consent of the publisher except in the case of brief quotations embodied in critical articles and reviews.

PRINTED BY CREATESPACE
an Amazon.com Company

www.timschoonard.com

Dedication:
To those who fought the Korean War; "the forgotten war" and your contribution to it has not been forgotten, and in gratitude to American fighting men and women everywhere.

AUTHORS NOTE TO READERS:

Please note that I have included a few "footnotes" in the text that have some additional or explanatory information that relates to the particular topic.

Also there are some military abbreviations that not all lay people may be familiar with, particularly:

PFC: Private First Class
CPL: Corporal
SGT: Sargent
LT: Lieutenant
CPT: Captain
LTC: Lieutenant Colonel
COL: Colonel
RCT: Regimental Combat Team, basically an infantry regiment augmented with other combat support units like artillery, medical, transportation, armor, etc. The basic infantry structure of a regiment consisted of three battalions, each consisting of four company sized units of various platoons and squads.
DIVISION: The 2nd Infantry Division incorporated the 9th, the 23rd, and the 38th Regimental Combat Teams, as well as other support units. Other United Nations units were adjoined to the Division units to augment their military strength.
ROK: Republic of Korea (U.N. Allied South Korean troops).
CCF: Chinese Communist Forces.

CONTENTS

Author's Introduction 9
Prologue: KOREA ON THE EVE OF WAR 13

I. THE INVASION OF INCHON 17
II. THE CALL OF A WARRIOR 23
III. FIRST COMBAT 33
IV. THE ALLIED DRIVE INTO NORTH KOREA 41
V. DUG IN AT "CHINAMAN'S HAT" 51
VI. REAR GUARD AT KUNU-RI 69
VII. SUICIDE RUN: ESCAPE FROM KUNU-RI 79
VIII. PRISONER OF WAR 85
IX. RIGHT BACK IN THE SADDLE 95
X. FIGHTING A WAR IN KOREA 103
XI. A BATTLEFIELD COMMISSION 123
XII. DIGGING IN AT CHIPYONG-NI 129
XIII. UNDER SIEGE 137
XIV. A TIME TO STAND OR DIE 151
XV. A MEDAL OF HONOR 161
XVI. A PURPLE HEART 177

Epilogue: LIFE GOES ON FOR THE WARRIOR 185

TESTIMONY TO A WARRIOR 195

Appendix: A QUEST FOR THE MEDAL OF HONOR 197

Historical References: 203

AUTHOR'S INTRODUCTION

I'm not sure how many recollections of the war have been written from the "foxhole-eye-view" of the combat soldier. Many are written after-the-fact by competent historians, or from a "Command" point of view by officers who may have been closely involved in the war effort, but rarely right on the front line. All are beneficial and worthy, but few share the intense personal experience of the individual soldier suffering under combat conditions and standing face to face with the enemy.

I have known Chester Thiessen for over 32 years. He has been both friend and often mentor during that time, and has taught me many life lessons that have benefitted my family and me for decades. The first time he began to share bits and pieces of his war memories with me, I listened with great interest.

Many in my own family had served in the military both in war and peacetime, and I've always had the greatest personal respect for veterans. Growing up during the Vietnam war watching Walter Cronkite talk about the war and give casualty statistics every night on the news made the anomaly of war, though I had scarce appreciation for what it all entailed, a normal part of everyday life for me. As a boy I used to ride my bike over to my great uncle's house and he would bring out his glass jars full of German insignia and lay them out on the table explaining what they were and of his (101st Airborne) and his brother's (82nd Airborne) actions in the "Battle of the Bulge", as well as his sufferings at Bastogne during WWII.

My own grandfathers served as well. One, both in the Navy during WWI, and the Army during WWII, and the other tried to enlist but had a health condition that prevented it, so he packed up and went east to build battleships in support of the war effort, years later using the skills learned to personally train many of the professional welders that built the Alaskan pipeline. My own father retired from the Army National Guard after more than 20 years of service. Needless to say, a patriotic spirit ran in my blood, and when Chet began to rather reluctantly share his memories, my fervor became a veritable pry bar of questions to learn about this war I knew so little about. What I didn't anticipate from his sharing of experiences with me is that I would be so inspired, I soon found myself, at 26, enlisted in the Army and on my way to Ft. Leonard Wood, Missouri for Basic Training.

Chet and I have had many long conversations about his Korean War experiences over the last 30 years, and the stories have always remained consistent. His integrity and reputation are well known and highly regarded. To preserve the experiences of a combat soldier during what is often coined "The Forgotten War" for the benefit of this and future generations, I decided I would embark, with Chet's permission, on this writing adventure.

I spent many hours interviewing and recalling shared memories with Chet to gather the core of this work. Unfortunately, due to combat conditions, lower ranked enlisted men didn't have the luxury of taking part in command briefings because they were normally on the line vigilantly sitting in a frozen foxhole watching for the ever present enemy, and didn't always know exactly where they were at any given time.

For the reader and flow of the story I have attempted to fill in between Chet's memories with accurate historical information about the war, gleaned from official army records and accounts written by historians and other personal memoirs of Korean War soldiers, to include sworn affidavits and eye witness testimonies. Many thanks go out to retired Lieutenant Colonel Sherman Pratt, who was Chet's Company Commander during most of his Korean service who had sent us a copy of his own memoirs, *Decisive Battles of the Korean War* that helped me to track the locations of Chet's particular unit from place to place amidst the larger overview provided by Army records and command reports.

I ask the patience of the reader with my artistic license concerning various military terminologies, as some of it has changed over the generations, especially my use of "cannon" in describing some artillery and tank weaponry. I did so intentionally because as I wrote the story, the incredulously tremendous artillery barrages sent forth in the Korean War against the massive Communist assaults reminded me continually of old sailing ships furiously firing their massive cannons point blank at each other. It was loud, violent, intentional, and above all, intensely personal. For the sake of my reader's perception and the dynamics of the action taking place, I think it an accurate description.

While I have used accurate historical information in the sharing of this story, my intent was not so much to paint a history lesson on the intricacies of the Korean War, as it was to share the unique and personal memories of one combat soldier, as seen *Through the Eyes of the Warrior*.

PROLOGUE:

KOREA ON THE EVE OF WAR

The Korean peninsula, resting between the Yellow Sea and Sea of Japan, is bordered on the North by both China and Russia. At the time Japan had occupied Korea, and after WWII the United Nations had dispersed control of the Korean territory between Russia, north of the 38th parallel, and the United States, south of the 38th parallel. In 1947 when the UN wanted to have an election to re-establish the Korean republic, Russia balked and did their own thing, while the Southern territory had its proposed democratic election, resulting in a

Communist controlled North Korea and a democratically governed South Korea.

The North Koreans, under Communist Russia developed a massive, well-equipped, and well-trained military force, while the South Koreans maintained a limited, police type military force augmented by UN security forces. Tensions and aggressions flared between the two until on June 25, 1950 the Russian trained and equipped North Korean Army crossed the 38th parallel into South Korea. Through September of 1950 the North Korean Army dominated the military action, pushing the South Koreans and their supporting UN forces almost to the ocean into a tight enclave south of the Naktong River around the coastal city of Pusan, where they held until U.S. and other UN forces were able to come to their aid.

On September 15, 1950 American forces landed at Inchon, near Seoul on the western shore of Korea just south of the 38th parallel, while at the same time, the American 8th Army crossed the Naktong, breaking out of the Pusan perimeter to the north, to push the North Korean Armies back to where they came from while the Inchon invasion north and west of them sought to cut their supply lines.

It is into this scenario we find the young soldier of this story, Chet Thiessen, a 17 year old replacement troop landing with the second wave at

Inchon, who had been transferred to the 2nd U.S. Infantry Division from the 101st Airborne.

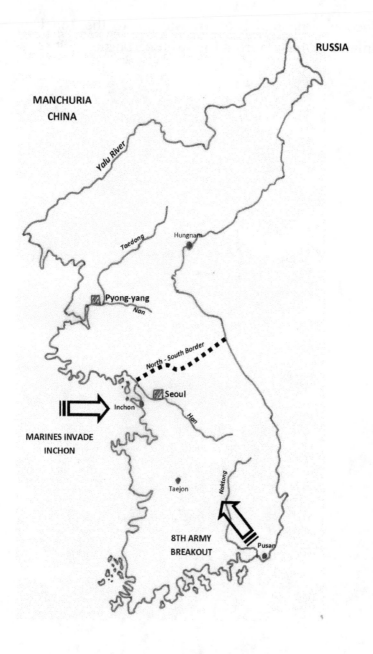

CHAPTER I

THE INVASION OF INCHON

Inchon Harbor, Just off the coast of Korea, Fall, 1950

"Over here, hurry! Get them in the boat before the sharks come!" Came a muffled shout from someone in the landing craft as the young soldier's head came up and broke through the water's surface. He shook his head to clear the salty brine from his eyes and gasped eagerly for air as he struggled to keep his face above water, kicking his feet madly away from the depths below. "Sharks?!" He shouted inside himself, "Wait - there's blood in the water - sharks. We were warned this bay was infested with them!" He never realized how hard it was to swim in a pair of combat boots. But Chet Thiessen had come all this way to fight a war; he wasn't about to be eaten by some fish!

Frantically reaching out to grab handfuls of blood red water with his right hand, he ungracefully pulled himself closer to the landing craft that was pitching up and down on the waves before him. In his other hand he firmly held what he had come for, the wounded officer who had suddenly fallen from the cargo netting on his way down the side of the ship to the landing craft. How the officer wasn't crushed to death between the side of the ship and the sturdy troop laden landing craft that pitched back and forth on the waves, slamming over and over into the unyielding iron of the troop ship's hull, he didn't know, but what amazed him even more, was that he too hadn't been crushed to death as well when he jumped in to save him! "What was I thinking about?" He asked himself.

Moments before, Chet Thiessen had been standing in the landing craft trying to steady himself against the constant pitching of the deck beneath his feet. It had been a long way down from the ships rail on that cargo net ladder. Climbing those darn rope ladders was a challenge when they were holding still, let alone when they were hanging from a pitching troop ship that is taking fire from the shore nearby. It felt good to him to be finally out of the line of fire and sheltered by the steel plate of the landing craft.

A scream from above had gotten Chet's attention and he saw the Lieutenant fall from the ladder and into the narrow strip of water that revealed itself for mere moments in one of the landing crafts regular sways away from the ship's hull as the sea pushed it hard against the lanyards that tethered it, until the same forces would pull it back again to slam against the side of the ship. At the time, he really didn't stop to think, he just took action. The sea water was murky; tinged with the red of the blood of the American soldiers who had landed ahead of them and whose dead bodies now littered the shore or bobbed silently, floating in the shallows near it. Chet quickly looked over the side and saw the gold bars of the officer glinting dimly in the sunlight nearly three feet under and sinking away. Before he knew it, he had tossed his helmet and rifle aside and leapt through the narrow gap that remained between the ship and the landing craft into the water after the officer.

Dozens of mighty arms sporting strong hands reached down and easily hauled them both back up over the side and into the landing craft. The injured Lieutenant's wounds were seen to, but Chet never found out what ever happened to him. He stood there shivering in the cool shadow of the steel walls, dripping wet as the blood tinged water puddled onto the deck at his feet, as if he had been strangely baptized somehow in this blood of the soldiers who had already given their lives to fight the battle he was soon to face himself.

From behind him, a big hand grabbed him by the shoulder sopping down on his wet uniform. "Man Chet, I thought you were a goner!" smiled his friend Bernie Cartee, as he handed him back his rifle and helmet. "You could have been squished like a bug, or worse yet, lunch." He teased.

All Chet could do at the moment was smile back and nod. He and Bernie had been good friends and soldiering together for some time. They started out together in Basic Training, and had ended up serving together in several units already, now here they were again. Chet tried to gather his wits as he donned his helmet, then checked his rifle closely and inspected his ammo. The last thing he needed was to get ashore and find all his bullets were lying on the bottom of the bay. This was going to be a long day.

The landing craft pilot and crew suddenly shouted commands back and forth as the last soldiers made it down the ladders. The lines were cast off and the engines roared to life as the vessel pulled away and headed for the battle worn shore.

Standing only four guys from the front door of the landing craft, Chet had been well trained in some of the toughest units in the Army, but was still a bit anxious realizing it wouldn't be a long ride in. Inchon harbor boasted some of the highest tides in the world and that made it possible for our ships to get in close to shore. The downside was that it was close enough for small arms fire to reach it. Like rocks thrown up against the side of a steel sided barn, the snap, snap of enemy rounds tapped against the landing craft hull as they plowed their way the short 400 yards in.

Above the soldiers heads, over the distant explosions caused of incessant airstrikes against the enemy positions, two fifty caliber machine guns roared as the Coast Guard gunners fired from the shelter of the shielded firing turrets of the landing craft, dishing out some intimidating suppression fire to force the enemy to keep their heads down and make it safer for the troops to dismount when they reached the more secure shore landing positions.

As the young soldier stood there waiting for what lay ahead, strangely, his thoughts went back to ponder all the events that had taken place in his life that brought him here to this moment.

CHAPTER II

THE CALL OF A WARRIOR

Chet Thiessen grew up in Grand Rapids, Michigan. His parents had separated before he was born, so he never knew his father until later in life. Though he took much from the solid examples shown him by his Grandfather and uncle, in the end it fell to his young shoulders to constantly make the choices that would decide for him the type of man he would grow to be in the future.

When he was in the third grade, Chet's cousin had returned home from the war in the Pacific, after being wounded at Guadalcanal. He asked his cousin if he would mind coming to his school and talking to his class. His cousin agreed and his teacher consented. The talk that he gave that day really made an impression on the curious young boy, an impression that would haunt him for years to come.

He hadn't made the conscious decision to become a soldier just then, but as a skinny little kid, without a father around, living in one of the roughest neighborhoods in Grand Rapids, fighting became somewhat of a normal daily activity. Much to his mother's distress, many a day he came home all bloody and bruised with his clothing ripped to shreds.

He didn't win too many of those fights, but that tenacious, skinny kid that stood his ground against much larger opponents and never backed down even when he was outnumbered eventually won the healthy respect of his schoolmates. This natural obstinacy and determination gleaned from the experiences of youth would come in real handy on many a frozen battlefield in the future.

"When I got to be about 15, something seemed to change in me. That's the only way I can describe it. I felt drawn to the military and joined the Michigan National Guard," Thiessen recounts.

When I was sixteen, I became very restless. I decided it was time to get out and see more of the world. I dropped out of school, lied about my age, and tried to enlist in the Marines. I took the physical and found out I was colorblind. So the Marine Corps shot me down.

I thought, well I'll try the Navy instead. But found they didn't want anyone who had colorblindness either, so same story."

Disappointed, but not one to give up easily, Chet gave it one last shot and tried the Army. He went to the Army recruiting station and asked if they had any problem with a guy being colorblind.

"Can you breathe?" the Recruiting Sergeant asked somewhat sarcastically.

"Sure," Chet answered proudly.

"Sign here kid, you're in the Army."

What had at first seemed to be a curse, would later prove to be a blessing as Chet found to his surprise that his colorblind condition would allow him to see enemy camouflage nearly as easily as "hunter orange," much to the dismay of many an enemy soldier.

Chet Thiessen travelled by train to Camp Funstun, Kansas, to undergo basic training with the 10th Mountain Division. After a pleasant trip down, he gathered outside the train with the others with him. A Drill Sergeant checked them in and informed them there were refreshments waiting at the mess hall.

"O.K. you wanna-be soldiers, gather up your crap and follow me. Cookie has some donuts and coffee waiting for you at the chow hall. I know you don't know how to march yet, and we'll soon fix that, so just try to stay in a line if you can and follow me."

The dozen or so new recruits straggled behind the Drill Sergeant to the mess hall, where the Mess Sergeant greeted them cordially.

"C'mon in boys, there's some donuts here for ya and paper plates over there. See them big shiny coffee urns? Hot coffee right there. Help yourselves."

The tenacious young man from the streets of Grand Rapids who wanted to be a soldier had acquired some habits that didn't exactly fit into the military way of doing things. After the group had finished eating, the Mess Sergeant pointed to four or five guys and asked them to clean up the mess hall before they left. The last of these was Chet, and from the expression on his face, the Sarge could tell Chet wasn't happy with his selection.

The Mess Sergeant asked Chet sternly, "So, what's the matter with you?"

"You can go to hell!"

"Oh, a smartass aye? Well I can take care of that. O.K. you guys, you can all get out of here," the Sarge gestured to Chet, who sat begrudgingly in his seat, "All except the smartass here."

After the new recruits had filed out behind the Drill Sergeant, the Mess Sergeant turned to Chet, "O.K. sonny boy, you're gonna clean this entire mess hall. Follow me."

Chet reluctantly followed the Sergeant to the kitchen. The impeccably shined and polished stainless steel fixtures were neatly stacked with mountains of pots, pans, eating trays, and other kitchen appointments. As Chet watched wide eyed, the Mess Sergeant proceeded to take his arm and cleared every single piece of the stacked pots, pans, trays and whatever was standing, from where they were stacked onto the kitchen floor with a crash.

As the new recruit looked with dismay at the mountain of stainless steel on the floor before him, the Mess Sergeant continued, "Now, I want all of these washed, dried, and stacked, just like we had them. When you're done with that, you see those things under the sinks there? Those are grease traps. I want them cleaned too. And don't forget to mop up the place. Everything you'll need is in that closet over there. Have a nice night, I'll be back to check on you in the morning."

Thus passed Chet Thiessen's first day in the Army. It was not the last of the "formative experiences" of Basic Training that would mold him first into a soldier and then into the warrior he would later become. When he finally reached graduation day, his Drill Sergeant, a combat hardened WWII vet, complemented Pvt. Thiessen jovially, "Thiessen, I think I've been hard enough on you to say I've put you through Basic Training twice in one trip!"

It was in Basic Training that Chet Thiessen first met Bernie Cartee.

"Bernie and I seemed to hit it off right away. He was a roughneck Native American, and was tough as nails. He was the kind of guy who would get into a fight at the drop of a hat – and he was always willing to be the one to drop the hat!" Chet recalled with a smile.

"One day Bernie and I saw a troop walk by wearing jump boots that had white shoelaces. For some reason those white laces really impressed us. We put in a request and both of us were soon TDY to Fort Campbell, Kentucky, assigned to the Screamin' Eagles of the 101st Airborne Division."

The tough training received by members of the 101st seemed to suit the two young men just fine. After 36 parachute jumps under all kinds of conditions, the pair suddenly got new orders. This time to a duty station where their paratroop skills wouldn't be needed, but their infantry skills would. Private First Class Chet Thiessen and Private First Class Bernard Cartee were bound by train for the northwest coast, where a ship awaited them.

After a short leave granted them to visit their families, late in the summer of 1950, a ship full of replacement troops bound for Korea, headed out for Japan from Fort Lawton, Washington.

"When we finally docked in Yokahama harbor, almost thirty days later, we took on supplies. The voyage over was peaceful. I actually got to see some real live whales once, swimming alongside our ship.

I remember standing on deck the day we arrived, and watching as hundreds of Japanese workers on the dock carried box after box of something on their shoulders into the ship. The long lines of men reminded me of an anthill there were so many. They would carry a box into a door on the side of the ship, and leave by another, a few seconds later. I asked an officer who by chance was passing by what they were loading. I thought they might be rations for all the men."

"Ammunition," He said."It was a cold reminder of where we were going. Any "peaceful" voyage we had enjoyed thus far would soon be over." As the tugboats came and pulled the ship from its moors out into open water, the Captain briefed the troops that they were now under radio silence conditions, enroute for Pusan. *"We arrived offshore of Pusan, where we knew our troops had had a hell of a time,"* remembered Chet, *"and we could see*

a lot of activity on the shore. But we didn't stop here. New orders came through and the ship kept going. We were now bound for Inchon, farther up the coast of the Korean peninsula where a new invasion had begun to join with our push from Pusan to form a type of circle around the North Koreans who had invaded the south and push them back north."

Later the ship steamed into Inchon harbor, amidst the battle noise in the distance as incessant sorties of aircraft pounded the enemy lines a few miles inland. Other air strikes hit closer targets to stifle the enemy that remained to fire upon the ships near the shore and the landing craft that brought in supplies and reinforcements to the base of American operations setting up near Inchon.

Laden with rifles and ammo, the soldiers anxiously waited on deck, shielded from the errant enemy small arms fire that pinged harmlessly against the steel structures of the ship, for the order to board the landing crafts that were moving in to collect them. Any other equipment they would need would be issued when they got to the operations base set up on shore.

Finally the order was given, and with practiced discipline, along with his fellow soldiers, Private First Class Chet Thiessen silently and dutifully moved to the rail, slung his rifle over his shoulder, and carefully maneuvered his way down the loose and shifting squares of the cargo net ladder to the awaiting landing craft tossing and swaying in the ocean below.

When his feet finally landed on the steel of the landing craft deck, he had to grab the side to steady himself. The small craft felt a lot different in the water than the ship he had spent the last month on. He looked around briefly at all of the activity around him and the faces of his fellow soldiers. But, before he had a chance to take in what was going on, he was distracted by a scream that rang out from the net ladder right above him . . .

CHAPTER III

FIRST COMBAT

The landing craft shuddered as it skidded to a halt on the shoreline. Seconds later the front gate fell and Chet Thiessen moved forward onto Korean soil for the first time.

There was little time to take in the surroundings. Amidst the shouts of the combat leaders, the men made a run across the short stretch of beach, so they wouldn't be shot at like sitting ducks. The beachhead had already been taken and secured, so there was no heavy resistance from dug in North Korean troops, but there was still real danger from sniper fire, a constant threat to anyone caught in the open.

The fresh soldiers made their tactical dash for the tree line not far in the distance, and PFC Thiessen took shelter in the shadow of a burned out building while he caught his breath. In moments, the men headed inland to the Army operations base nearby.

When Chet and Bernie Cartee reached the operations base, they were met by an officer who directed them to the "RepoDepo" or Replacement Depot, where they would be assigned to the units that were in need of replacement troops for other soldiers who had been wounded or killed. At the Replacement Depot, PFC Thiessen was pulled aside by an Officer.

"Thiessen, we saw what you did back there, diving in that hellhole water to save that Lieutenant. That was certainly above and beyond the call of duty. He's lucky to be alive, and so are you. We're putting you in for the Bronze Star. Good job soldier."

While no Bronze Star medal ever materialized, Thiessen and Cartee, along with about 25 others, were assigned to the 2nd Infantry Division, also known as the "Warrior" or "Indianhead" Division whose unit patch was proudly represented by an American Indian chieftain in full feathered headdress across a white star against a black shield, who were dug in many miles ahead. The group of replacements all went to gather the equipment they would need to face the combat conditions that waited.

"Hey Chet, it looks like we'll be trading in our Screamin' Eagles for the Indian Head. It's about time my people got some credit!" Cartee joked.

"Yeah, yeah, you got that right 'Chief'!" Chet jabbed back.

The detachment set out for the 2nd Division positions on the front line. By the time they made the ten mile trek it was coming dark. Long before they arrived, the sounds of war greeted them, as continuous air strikes of naval aircraft bombed, rocketed, and strafed the enemy positions in the distance. They came upon the headquarters of Able Company and reported in.

The officer that greeted them informed the group, "You men are assigned to Baker Company. We can't get you there until morning; they're currently pinned down out there and under heavy fire. We can't get through at night."

The Mess Sgt. saw them coming in, and asked them all if they had eaten. "Get on in here and get some hot chow boys. You've got a big day ahead of you tomorrow."

After a grateful meal in the field mess, they were shown where they could sleep for the night.

"I remember that first night there. You could hear the sounds of small arms fire all over the place, and see the Napalm lighting up the night and exploding in massive fiery balls in the distance," reminisced Thiessen, *"But in spite of all that, strangely, I slept peacefully that night."*

The next morning finally came. They cautiously made their way to the B Company position, where the men were met by a Platoon Sergeant.

The Sgt. asked Chet, "Thiessen, your paperwork says you know how to handle a machine gun?"

"Yes sir," he answered confidently, not sure why he was asking. He had really taken to the .30 caliber machine gun during infantry training, and his skills had earned him the additional MOS.

"We sure can certainly use that." He gestured, "I need you to stop over at that bunker over there and pick up a thirty cal. Cartee, I am assigning you to him as ammo bearer. Both of you are assigned to 3rd Platoon, Heavy Weapons squad.

Pfc. Thiessen, I know it's your first day, but as the machine gunner, you're the new squad leader. Welcome to Korea "Corporal." Your squad is over there along that ridgeline. You'll find them dug in in a bunker. The enemy is over yonder. Trip flares should already be set in front of your position. Field phones are in. Keep somebody close to yours at all times, and keep an eye on the wires. Somebody will be checking in with you later. Tonight a full moon will be out. The Reds like to attack at night, and they love a full moon. They'll be coming tonight, guaranteed. Any questions?"

"No sir."

"Grab your rations before you move out. Stay sharp, men. Carry on."

At six-foot-two and 150 pounds, Cpl. Chet Thiessen, as possibly the lightest man in his unit, was not the one you would have expected to see assigned to bear the heft of the air-cooled .30 caliber machine gun. But toughened by the rigorous training of the 101st Airbourne, he welcomed the extra firepower.

The two men cautiously struggled their way up the rough terrain to an open bunker on top of the ridge. After introductions to the other six men who would make up the squad, Chet Thiessen set up his machine gun position, inspected the weapon, loaded it and arranged the canvas ammo belt so it wouldn't get twisted, then together with his new squad, anxiously watched over their position for signs of enemy activity.

Chet Thiessen recounts that first day: *"We were situated on the ridge in an open bunker, and though it had been a hot and sweaty day in the summer heat, it began to rain. It rained for hours, but we were able to stay mostly dry under our ponchos. After taking that dive in the bay from the landing craft, I had barely dried out before the rain came and I got wet all over again.*

ATTACK ALWAYS AT FULL MOON

When night came we were on high alert. Finally the rain stopped and the clouds began to clear, letting the light of the full moon through to light up everything. We had two trip flares go off in front of our position, and the enemy was suddenly right there. We held our ground and fought most of the night, and I'm pretty sure I burned up at least one box of ammo.

When the sun came up I saw at least 20 dead North Korean soldiers lying out in front of our position. The order came to move out and we began to advance on the next ridge ahead. As we moved forward, we started to take heavy fire. I saw guys dropping all around me."

The air was alive with explosions, fire and smoke, screams of soldiers wounded and dying, and hot lead from both friendly and enemy fire as the 2nd Division advanced amidst constant waves of

Navy planes that hammered the enemy positions with napalm, rockets, and strafing. Surprisingly, even with the muffled ringing in his ears caused from the deafening noise made by the rhythmic thunder erupting from the short bursts of his .30 caliber machine gun he fired from the hip, it didn't take the young Squad Leader long to get used to the battle noise, and he was able to focus on leading his squad forward.

"The enemy fire had driven our squad into a rice paddy area and was keeping our heads down. Until we heard the explosion, we didn't know we were stuck in the middle of a mine field. One of my guys had gotten his leg blown off below the knee. Another of my men was able to get to him and carry him out. I remember shouting to him to stay in his same footprints on the way out."

The newly appointed Corporal Thiessen successfully led his squad forward where the Regiment took the next ridge from the enemy, and proceeded to dig in to hold it. Thus went Corporal Chet Thiessen's first day in combat. He was 17 years old.

40

CHAPTER IV

THE ALLIED DRIVE INTO NORTH KOREA

A successful United Nations amphibious invasion by the United States 10th Corps and allied forces at Inchon, near Seoul, fought to cut off the enemy supply lines while another counteroffensive was initiated by UN forces, including the 23rd Regimental Combat Team of the 2nd Infantry Division, breaking out for the north across the Naktong River from the UN stronghold near Pusan.

After landing at Inchon and joining up as replacements for the brutally combat worn and decimated ranks of the 23rd Regimental Combat Team (RCT), Thiessen and Cartee joined in the heroic and savage daily battles fought by the advancing U.N. forces. Much like his first day in combat, Chet Thiessen described each day as just another attempt to take the next ridgeline in front of them held by the enemy. Day in and day out the men of Baker Company of the 1st Battalion fought along with the other units for every inch of bloody ground taken as the 8th Army struggled to push the Communist North Korean forces back northward and across the 38th parallel that signified the border between North and South Korea.

Once the 8th Army began to show its teeth and pierce through the North Korean forces, most of the enemy began a rapid retreat north that found the friendly forces fighting and taking ground at a rapid pace. At one point, the 38th Regimental Combat Team of the 2nd Division advanced 77 miles in only 10 hours, crashing roadblock after roadblock, until finally having to stop because their vehicles had run out of gas.

By October 1, 1950, it was announced that there was no longer any organized resistance from the enemy forces, and all of them except for a few straggler units had been pushed back across the 38th parallel from whence they had come.

Finally and thankfully, at this time the 2nd Division forces were able to stand down for a short while and get some much needed rest, have a chance to re-group, re-supply, and get any needed medical treatment, while at the same time, pulling everything together with a look to the near future.

The respite wasn't to last long; a new mission was being planned.

On the 17th of October operation "Indianhead" was initiated, driving forward in a high-speed, three pronged spearhead determined to take the North Korean capital of Pyongyang. The force met little resistance, and on October 19th the first of the allied forces rolled into Pyongyang. The greatest obstacle they encountered to taking the city wasn't enemy

troops, but the Taedong River that passed through the center of town, with apparently no way across. Small groups were able to cross in assault boats, and some smaller vehicles eventually made it across a railroad bridge. Finally, the tanks and other large vehicles were able to find a crossing at a point up river. But, in spite of the challenges, by the end of the day the entire city of Pyongyang belonged to the United Nations forces.

The rapid surge north had strained the allied forces supply trains to the limit. Almost every item that was needed now had to be sent by truck hundreds of miles over the narrow dirt "highway" that wound its way through the mountainous territory, or dropped by air. To address the problem, the famous "Red Ball Express" was formed. It consisted of over 300 trucks running flat out, twenty-four-seven, up and down the Seoul-Pyongyang highway to make continuous supply runs of everything needed for combat support.

Near the end of October, reports were coming in from our allied forces of the Republic of Korea (ROK) who were operating farther north, that they were being attacked off and on by Chinese Communist units. By October 31st, our intelligence had revealed that 316,000 Chinese troops had gathered at the Manchurian border between China and North Korea. This vast array of troops equaled 44 units the size of the 2nd Infantry Division. This amounted to the equivalent of 12 full Chinese "Armies", compared to our one 8th Army fighting there in Korea.

There was no information available to reveal the intentions of the massive forces gathered on the other side of the border with Communist China, and until such time as there was, the allied forces were determined to continue their march northward.

The Chinese

November arrived with disturbing news. The 1st and 2nd ROK Corps, at the northern front, began taking massive assaults that were forcing them to withdraw again and again, resulting in a situation that placed the 8th Army flank in danger. The 2nd Division was ordered to the Sunchon area to reinforce the line. Since most of its trucks were being used for the "Red Ball Express" supply train, this was difficult to accomplish.

The 2nd Division had barely moved into its new position when later the same day orders came attaching them to I Corps and giving them the responsibility of securing the areas to the rear of the lines, and patrolling south of the town of Kunu-ri a few miles north of Sunchon. At the same time, the 1st ROK and the 1st Cavalry Division were on the front lines ahead of them beginning to take heavy assaults from units of both North Korean and now surprisingly, some Chinese Communist Forces (CCF).

Aerial reconnaissance flights reported on November 2nd that large masses of enemy troops were moving toward Tokchon, east of Kunu-ri. The

2nd Division had been moved into position west of Kunu-ri and ordered to protect the right flank of I Corps at all cost.

Intelligence gathered from a Chinese prisoner gave surprising news. A force of 50,000 CCF troops had crossed the Yalu River on the Manchurian border and was now in Korea. The next day, the 2nd Division was transferred from the I Corps to the IX Corps after intelligence reported that eight North Korean Divisions along with large CCF units were building up in the area between Tokchon and Yongwon west of Kunu-ri.

At this point the 23rd RCT had been given the job of patrolling the areas south and east of Sunchon. Chet Thiessen was part of a patrol that made it into the town of Yangdok, where it discovered over 16 railroad cars full of fuel and ammunition stockpiled by the enemy. An even more startling discovery were large machine shops outfitted with tooling to make parts for Russian made weapons set up in underground mineshafts there.

"I remember these huge underground machine shops we found." Chet recalled, "The place was also stocked to the ceiling with hundreds of crates of Russian Vodka."

Demolition teams were called in and any ammo and other supplies not needed by the ROK troops were blown up.

In the days that followed, all of the units of the 2nd Division were set to patrolling searching out signs of the anticipated build-up of enemy troops, however very little evidence was found. Finally, east of Pukchang-ni the first Division fire fight with some random CCF units took place on or about November 10th.

On November 11th, the 9th RCT of the 2nd Division was ordered to take Pugwan and the surrounding hills along the Ch'ongchon river to the west. The enemy put up a tremendous fight, and the battle ran on for several days. By the 14th, the 9th RCT had taken the city and crossed the Ch'ongchon where it hooked up with friendly forces north of there.

Friendly patrols continued, but little enemy activity was found. An attack was planned by allied forces to curtail or crush any enemy build-up of troops to the north. But things began to heat up. Reports began to come in that enemy units were being found far to the south, well below and behind the Division Command post. The 9th RCT reported in that they were being hit hard by small units of CCF forces attacking the I Corps areas. Allied attack plans were put in motion on November 18th, while at the same time the 23 RCT were reporting in that North Korean enemy troops had infiltrated far to the south near Kapyong-ni. The 2nd Division

Command moved to an area just north and east of Kunu-ri in preparation for the Allied offensive.

By November 20th, the Division CP became inundated with a flood of reports of enemy activity and troop build-ups. In Heochang far to the southwest of Kunu-ri, an entire North Korean Division was discovered. Another mass of 12,000 enemy forces were reported to the southeast. Later, an additional 1,000 CCF troops were reported to be in Heochang as well, along with a ROK report that they had encountered three CCF regiments south of Yongwon. In spite of the harrowing news, following orders, the 2nd Division readied for their offensive to counter the troop build-up.

23 November, 1950 Thanksgiving Day. In what could be considered a logistical and tactical miracle, General MacArthur made good on his promise that all his troops would have a hot turkey dinner with all the trimmings on Thanksgiving Day. However in spite of this unusual extravagance, our allied soldiers did not get to spend the rest of the day sipping hot cider by a warm fire. Though with a full belly, CPL Chet Thiessen would continue security patrols with the 23rd RCT, staged in Kunu-ri as Division reserve, while the rest of the 2nd Division broke out in their drive north the very same day.

They encountered very little enemy resistance as they moved forward, though the next day, aerial recon reported large masses of enemy troops forming in front of the Division lines, but assuming the Chinese were just trying to create a deterrent to keep the UN forces from continuing on into China, and that they would withdraw as the North Korean forces already had ahead of the advancing UN forces, the Allied troops marched onward. That night, all was quiet.

CHAPTER V

DUG IN AT "CHINAMAN'S HAT"

The Manchurian winds fiercely blew their hell of subzero temperatures down on our troops dug in almost to the border of China. For the combat soldier out in the open it meant long, endless suffering nights of freezing cold like most people would never experience or imagine. It had been unclear the intentions of the massing Chinese forces in the border area, but our troops would soon get a glimpse at what they were.

On November 25th, Baker Company was sent nearly 20 miles east of Kunu-ri deployed again in Division reserve, and were dug in on a defensive line near the village of Kujang-dong across a cornfield west of the base of a hill nicknamed "Chinaman's Hat" that loomed in the distance to their right. With Able Company on their left flank covering the line between their position and the Ch'ongchon River, they held a reserve defensive, with the 61st Field Artillery about 300 yards in front of them, and the 9th Infantry on the front line, yet a mile farther out than that. Baker Company was staged to move forward to attack through the positions of the 9th the next day. Though diligent and prepared, except for some far off sounds of combat elsewhere on distant fronts, it had all been eerily quiet the last two days.

Finally darkness descended on the battlefield, the total blackness of a cold moonless night. Temperatures plunged to more than 20 below zero. As the soldiers of the allied forces hunkered down in their fighting positions for the night, rumors had been spreading like wildfire that because the allied offensive had been so successful in driving the North Koreans back, that the action may soon be over and some may be even home by Christmas, just a few weeks away.

It was then, just before midnight, the Chinese Communist Forces attacked. In a surprise attack that hit units of the 9th Infantry so hard and so fast that many didn't even have time to fire a shot, the Chinese attacked in overwhelming numbers totally overrunning the 9th RCT frontal positions as well as the 61st Field Artillery, forcing them to abandon their 105mm Howitzers intact. Moving fast, the mammoth Chinese force had swarmed over, around, and through, reaching the Baker Company line. The few random cornstalks that still stood in front and around their positions suddenly began to dance and splinter as the f-f-ft!, f-f-ft! of a torrent of small arms fire ripped through the air at Baker's position. A voice screamed out of the darkness, "The gooks are everywhere!", and Baker Company found itself face to face with a massive wave of Chinese troops. The infantry unit's careful fire mowed them down like grass, and though literal piles of bloody corpses piled up in front of their position, the outright slaughter didn't even seem to faze the fanatic, wild horde, who continued to rush forward with what seemed like an endless number of enemy soldiers.

Chet Thiessen recalls: *"I had enemy dead bodies stacked several high in front of my machine gun position. They just kept running up and over the pile at us! At first we thought they were North Korean, but later, when I had to go out and pull several of our wounded to safety, I noticed the different uniforms."*

All across the allied front spread miles across the Korean peninsula, the vast hordes of the Chinese slammed, overrunning units everywhere. Baker fought bravely, firing point blank into the mass of enemy who were so close they were falling dead on top of our own soldiers. Suddenly, the attack began to subsist, and finally the enemy withdrew, almost as fast as they appeared.

After midnight, another wave hit, this time preceded by hundreds of enemy soldiers blowing whistles, horns, ringing bells and even what sounded like banging of pots and pans, making a horrendous din. Baker Company again fought fiercely, and the piles of enemy dead in front of their foxholes mounted. Finally, once again, the battlefield slowly fell silent.

All through the night, battered soldiers of the 9th Infantry and 61st Field straggled out of the darkness through the Baker Company line. Nearly frozen to death, missing helmets, shoes, and weapons, these exhausted and wounded men were tended to.

"I remember a lot of the guys bare feet were black with frostbite by the time they got to us."

By early the next day, the 9th RCT of the Division had taken heavy casualties and to accommodate for the losses, Chet Thiessen moved out along with his unit of the 1st Battalion, to help reinforce the 9th's right flank, a few miles north of the town of Kujang-dong. The town of Tokchon to the east had fallen to the enemy before noon. This meant the 38th RCT was in trouble now as the only escape route for their withdrawal had been the road through Tokchon, and now the rest of the 23rd RCT had to struggle to hold their line near Kujang-dong to provide the only other escape route of withdrawal for their 38th RCT to make a run laterally behind and across the front lines.

The next night, out of the darkness, the Chinese mobs swarmed against and over the 23rd positions. At 2115 hours, a force of 300 Chinese overran the 23rd RCT command post, some distance behind the front line. Both the 1st and 2nd Battalions were driven back several hundred yards, in savage combat until many were out of ammunition.

Near midnight on the 26th, the incessant attacks by the Chinese had overrun and pushed the 9th RCT back east and south of the Ch'ongchon, their assault with 3.5" rockets and recoilless rifles forcing many men into the frigid waters for cover. Those that survived the ordeal would later crawl from the arctic cold water in ice covered, frozen uniforms. As the units all scrambled to prepare for another attack, the enemy seemed to withdraw as quickly as they had come.

Ringing clearly through the cold blackness, out in the distance on the lower slopes of "Chinamen's Hat" the bugles, whistles, and banging of pans could be heard, while thousands of lights could be seen moving in the distance. The enemy was happy to let them know they controlled the high ground, and that there were a lot of them. The allied troops would be sitting ducks if the enemy brought their artillery to bear from those heights when the morning dawned. But allied forces weren't ready to run off just yet.

The furious onslaught brought by the Chinese had spoiled any hopes of Christmas at home for anyone. All hell had now broken loose, and every man realized a new chapter was beginning to be written in this war, and that the outcome was far from certain.

As daylight cleared the horizon, the friendly forces worked to unravel the details of the situation. The 23rd RCT headquarters easily walked back in to take back the command post they had lost only hours before. In another strange event of "combat" fate, the 61st Field Artillery troops that were able, later marched back through the Baker line and reclaimed their 105's that were found intact and ready to fire that morning. The enemy for some reason ignored the weapons in their night assaults, and now the 61st had them all back.

The commanders on the ground saw that an attack on the "Hat" was necessary to assure the enemy did not continue their advantage. Securing the high ground in the area became imperative. Company C marched out in a probing attack to recon the enemy positions. They had barely started up the slopes of the Hat when they found what they were looking for. Suddenly pinned down under overwhelming and murderous fire, they were stuck. Artillery and air strikes commenced, while tank units hammered the Hat slopes with cannon and .50 caliber machine gun fire, to bring relief to the Charlie Company situation.

"*From our position,*" *said Thiessen,* "*we could see the air strikes happening. At the time we weren't under any kind of fire and had opportunity to watch the planes flying. The Mustang's would zoom in fast with guns blazing, then tip their wings to drop their loads of Napalm, and pull up and away as fast as possible above the huge fiery explosion. The F-80's were bombing too, and they would drop and pull straight up like a rocket. We thought the enemy must have had some good communications set up because as soon as our F-80 jets came it wasn't long before there were some Russian MIG's in the air. The whole thing was quite a show; the only bad part was that we would soon be out there in the middle of all that.*"

The cold weather had been causing other dangerous problems in addition to the overwhelming swarms of the Chinese. Many of our troops weapons had either frozen up or wouldn't work properly because the lubricant used on the weapons became so thick the parts wouldn't move well enough for the bolts to move or the firing pins to make contact with the bullets with enough force to fire.

"While we got ready for our advance we took time to search the dead enemy for intelligence related items. On the Chinese, besides the sack of rice they carried around their necks, we found small metal tins of what looked like grease in their pockets. We had no idea what this was, but later found out it was Whale Oil. This is what the enemy used to lubricate their weapons in the freezing temperatures to keep them from freezing up. Frozen or sluggish acting weapons were a big problem for us, and a lot of us started using the whale oil – we always had a lot of it, thanks to the piles of enemy bodies lying around – and it really helped a lot with the problem."

Not long later, after being resupplied with ammo and rations, Baker Company moved out under clear, cold skies with elements of the 2nd Battalion, to join Charlie Company in the fight. Coming up on Charlie's left flank, it wasn't long before Baker Company was also pinned down, amidst the now bar-b-cued bodies of some freshly napalmed enemy, and under heavy small arms and mortar barrages. Command now instructed Baker to hold fast, and to not risk any more casualties because of the enemy being found to be present in far greater strength, providing much more resistance than ever anticipated. It would soon be time to pull back and regroup.

Baker and the other units held their ground throughout that day and the next night, where again the bitter cold returned. Casualties were carefully evacuated and supplies were spread around. Throughout the night and into the next day, Baker and the units of the 2nd Division were engaged in bitter fighting. In an attempt to consolidate forces, most of the 9th Regiment was wiped out as it waded across the Ch'ongchon river. The remnant survivors struggled from the rivers freezing waters to join up with the 23rd RCT First Battalion. As they braced for the next engagement, the enemy again strangely disappeared from the battlefield. Even the 23rd Regimental CP that had been overrun the day before was able to be re-occupied by the 23rd regimental command.

Commanders on the ground at the front were worried. Higher commanders didn't seem to grasp the seriousness of the problem, which was initially outside of everyone's comprehension. The fear was that there were far more Chinese involved than ever imagined. How thousands of enemy moving across the border went undetected to the air reconnaissance was unknown.

By noon on November 28th, against the overwhelmingly larger enemy force it was clear that the Division could never hold the line as planned. Heavy enemy assaults were hitting other allied units all across the front. The 2nd ROK Corps on the 2nd Division flank were all but wiped out, along with the Turkish units backing them up. The enemy was pouring through their sector poised to get behind friendly lines and surround them. The word finally came down for Baker Company and other units to pull back.

The remnants of the 9th RCT moved out on trucks provided by the 23rd RCT to Won-ni between Kujang-dong and Kunu-ri to set up a defense, the rest of the evacuating units could pass through. The 38th RCT, though terribly battered, withdrew to take up new positions northeast of Kunu-ri, escaping behind the defensive fire of the 23rd RCT who did everything they could to slow down the massive human wave attacks of the enemy.

The withdrawal operation placed every vehicle bumper to bumper in a slow exodus on the narrow Kujang-dong-Kunu-ri highway. Chinese units attacked the rear of the slow moving convoy:

"There was only one main road that everyone had to use. The 8th Army was retreating, and all of the troops, trucks, and armor had to use the same road, that was also plugged with Korean refugees fleeing south as well. It was a congested mess and slow going. At one point, I could see one of the refugee women lying in the ditch by the side of the road. She was all alone, and screaming as she struggled to give birth, while everyone else was running for their lives. It was at least ten below zero.

I could see from my position several of our ambulances creeping along near the rear of the column. I could only watch, in disbelief, as I saw several groups of Chinese soldiers running on foot to catch up to the ambulances, pull open the back doors, drag out the stretchers, and massacre all of our wounded one by one."

While the Chinese forces attacked the rear of the convoy, the expert rear guard action of the 23rd RCT prevented extreme damage to the Divisions units that were withdrawing. Shortly after midnight on November 29th, both Able and Baker Company (CPL Thiessen's unit) were deployed for the fifth time in the savage rear guard effort, all while the entire First Battalion of the 23rd was under a continuous nightmarish barrage of mortar and artillery fire sent by the onrushing Chinese hordes.

The 23rd RCT finally pulled back and joined the defensive line to the right of the 9th position west of the Won-ni area. The Divisions rapid withdrawal in the midst of the savage attacks of the Communist mobs had cost them big in both men and equipment. The tattered remains of the Indianhead Division couldn't dig in because the ground was frozen and little cover or concealment existed. But, digging in wasn't an option anyway, because the malice of the enemy was upon them as soon as they reached their new positions.

Confusion reigned in the ranks, the allied troops were beyond exhaustion, and many combat leaders were dead or wounded. Everyone valiantly did the best they could to follow orders and get the job done:

"I remember the withdrawal to Kunu-ri. It was total chaos, total confusion. I guess the best way to describe it was some kind of 'organized' chaos. In spite of all that was happening, we somehow got the job done. What was happening is not easy to put into words."

Because of the overwhelming amount of enemy troops bearing down on their positions, a withdrawal was begun by the 23rd Regiment who were slated to cover the withdrawal of the 2nd Division. Able and Baker Companies were to set up at the roadblock at Won-ni, about 10 miles south down the Kujang-dong-Kunu-ri road, relieving the 9th RCT in providing a defensive position all other units could pass through. The entire 8th Army was engaged in what would become a massive, bloody, and costly withdrawal ahead of innumerable thousands of Chinese troops.

Baker Company dug in at Won and set up their side of the road block as the battered, exhausted, UN troops made their way through the protective defenses in a haphazard, bumper to bumper column that stretched on all through the day and into the night toward Kunu-ri. The effects of the fierce combat endured shown clearly on the faces of the withdrawing troops, many whom staggered by in the crippling cold, wounded, and without helmets, weapons, or other gear.

The distinctive sounds of small arms and the b-r-r-r-p of enemy "burp" guns rang out in the crisp, cold air. All along the column the Chinese would fire from the ditches and hills along the road, harassing and sniping at the evacuating masses with small arms and grenades, sometimes rushing in small groups from the brush at the edge of the road to attack the beleaguered soldiers. The roadsides were strewn with dead and wounded soldiers and civilians as masses of Korean refugees intermixed with the troops, trying to escape the tragedy of war that raged all around them.

The evacuating units would fire back at the enemy, but never stopped to make a frontal stand against them, even the tanks in the column would fire into the enemy positions, but they never stopped moving. The fighting raged continually, and along with the 1st Battalion, Baker Company was deployed over and over in rear guard fighting against the continually advancing Chinese forces.

"Get down! Get down!" Shouted someone, as all the troops in earshot instinctively threw themselves flat on the ground or dove behind any type of protective cover, as enemy machine gun fire erupted from a hidden bunker nearby. The surprised cries of two American soldiers were immediately silenced as they died in the spray of lead before their exhausted bodies even hit the ground.

"Man, we've got to get out of here!" Corporal Thiessen shouted to PFC Anderson and Cartee who kept right on his heels with their machine gun tripod and boxes of ammo to feed the always hungry weapon.

"Chet, if the convoy gets backed up again, everyone will be sitting ducks real soon!" Cartee shouted back, the extreme anxiety in his voice not hiding his emotions.

"I've got an idea, quick, follow me!" Thiessen motioned with his head. The three men, crouched low, ran quickly forward to a small pile of logs and brush nearby. Gasping for breath amidst the roar of gunfire from the Chinese bunker not far away that was doing a good job of keeping the rest of Baker Company pinned down, and wiping the sweat from his eyes with the back of his mitten. "Give me a fresh belt."

Roy Anderson with practiced precision had another belt of ammo out of the ammo box at his side and loaded in the machine gun in seconds.

"When I give the word, cover me, and shoot like hell at those muzzle flashes from the bunker. They've got company coming!" Ordered Thiessen. "NOW!"

Bernie Cartee and Roy Anderson carefully and quickly raised up just enough to fire over the log pile in front of them, laying down rhythmic and carefully spaced cover fire upon the narrow opening of the enemy bunker, with the intention of keeping the enemies heads down before they found out Chet was heading their way. Thiessen darted from the other end of the log pile creating a careful side angle to the enemy bunker, just out of their line of site, but giving him clear view of where they were firing from. His heart racing from both terror and exhaustion he ran toward the bunker and opened up with the .30 caliber. In mere seconds that seemed like hours, he screamed and charged forward as the stream of fire lit with the glow of tracer rounds reached out like a fiery spear to tear and shred everything around the opening in the enemy bunker. In their surprise, the enemy soldiers ceased their fire for a moment, then resumed with new fury.

As Chet Thiessen neared the bunker he could see an enemy soldier pop up from somewhere near the back of the bunker, looking right in his direction. Apparently the tracer trail from his .30 had tipped off what direction he was coming from. As he watched in horror, the same enemy soldier tossed a dark object in his direction.

"Grenade!" His own voice screamed in his head, and he dove for a shallow depression in the ground a few feet away, but not before the feared deafening blast erupted in a shower of deadly shrapnel, fire, and smoke. Corporal Thiessen hit the ground amidst the cloud of smoke, as clumps of dirty snow, rocks, and ice rained down upon him. He landed hard in the frozen depression, but not before shrapnel had hit him causing flesh wounds in his legs and hands. Bleeding, but ignoring the pain, adrenalin and panic taking over, he kept rolling over until he came up on one knee facing the bunker. Wet dirt coating his uniform, concealed by the smoke that was still clearing he let loose a short burst from his weapon and shot the enemy soldier who threw the grenade, who stood curiously watching in anticipation of the damage his grenade had done.

The soldier let out a surprised yip as his torso exploded in a shower of red before he disappeared from sight. Corporal Thiessen ran to where the soldier had fallen and found the hole that served as the bunker door. A flurry of enemy fire was still pouring out at the friendly troops retreating down the road toward Kunu-ri. Still half a belt of ammo left, Thiessen hosed down the inside of the bunker with a spray of lead, greeted by the anticipated screams of the dead and dying. The few survivors in the bunker fired at him through the back door opening, and he dodged aside while at the same time reaching for a grenade of his own. With one smooth motion he pulled the pin with his teeth, let the spoon fly, and tossed the grenade into the bunker. There was a flash, a loud noise, a cloud of smoke, and all fell silent. 11 Chinese soldiers now lay dead before him. The bunker now silenced, without a word the troops continued their move forward. This terrible day, this was just business as usual.

The focus of the 8th Army withdrawal, though unforeseen, costly, and confusing, was tactical; the intention was to get the hell out while it was still possible, and later re-assess and regroup to fight again. Any delay would certainly increase the casualty count and may make it impossible to get out. Why the enemy didn't hit the remnants of the shattered friendly units as they had before was a mystery that would be later unveiled when the evacuating 23rd RCT would discover a heap of them ready to do business with the 2nd Division farther up the road.

As night fell on 28 November, again the Manchurian winds joined with the darkness in sending merciless cold temperatures on the solemn scene, the enemy's harassing actions continued, and the men of Baker Company made their stand, doing their best to keep up sporadic defensive fire at unseen targets to protect the last of the evacuating column, as enemy fire fell randomly in unpredictable spurts upon the bloody, grim exodus.

Nobody slept. It had been several days of non-stop combat with nothing more than a few disturbed and anxious cat-naps during the daylight hours. Dark, hollow eyes, painfully squinted into the night from dirty, gaunt, unshaven faces searching for enemy movement. The pain from the intense cold was indescribable, on top of bruises, torn muscles, colds, flu, and encroaching frostbite on faces, hands, and feet. Finally, just before morning dawned on November 29th, Able and Baker Companies were told to pull back to Kunu-ri, another 10 miles further down the road.

The 23rd RCT units received notice that it was to continue to serve as rear guard for its own 2nd Division, who was now covering as rear guard for the withdrawal of the 8th Army. All morning long the 2nd Infantry Division held off the enemy that outnumbered them. Word came through that a roadblock had been established by the enemy on the Kunu-ri-Sunchon road – the only way out. While units were deployed to take out the roadblock, the regimental combat teams were wearing down. Already exhausted, now many of the men were dead or wounded and in need of medical attention. Ammo was almost gone, and little other supplies remained. What was left of the units was weakening by the moment.

By 1700, attempts to remove the roadblocks had been unsuccessful. But the 23rd and the 38th holding positions south of Kunu-ri were given the order to pull back. The 38th had yet to evacuate across the Namdae River bridge just south of Kunu-ri, and one Company of the 23rd was to stay behind and protect it.

CHAPTER VI

REAR GUARD AT KUNU-RI

As the weary Baker Company made their way back to Kunu-ri, after several days of non-stop combat without let-up or rest, though on the verge of complete physical collapse, the troops had managed the several mile forced march with the Chinese on their heels. Just after nightfall, the haggard remnants of Baker Company silently wandered in tactical formation through the moonlit streets of Kunu-ri, and across the bridge spanning the Namdae River. The dark, battle damaged buildings and huts of Kunu-ri stared back at them in eerie silence as each soldier passed, focused on the

rhythmic crunch of the bitterly cold snow beneath numb feet as they pushed themselves forward; their tired bodies screaming out for rest they could not afford to give them. Not yet.

The last day and a half had seen both Able and Baker companies deployed at least five times in rear guard action. After several days of incessant combat, frozen water, frozen rations, and no sleep, they now looked more like dazed, adrenalin fueled zombies than the tough, combat ready soldiers they were just days before.

Back at what was the new defensive perimeter south of Kunu-ri, the situation was becoming more desperate by the hour. What had been Battalion strength units straggled in, exhausted, and did their best to set up defensive positions. The enemy roadblocks to the south on the planned escape route were still holding. Staying would soon mean certain death for the entire Division. They were trapped.

The 8th Army exit had been successful, and most of these elements, consisting of tens of thousands of vehicles bumper to bumper jamming the road for miles, were now rolling in to Pyongyang, about a hundred miles south of them. The heroic stands by units of the 2nd had effectively protected the 8th Army withdrawal. Now it was their turn to pull out to safer territory. Finally, the Commanding General sent the order to them to prepare to evacuate by way of the Kaechon-Sunchon highway. The 23rd RCT was ordered to stand and cover the rest of the Divisions withdrawal. They would stay behind to block the enemy advance while the rest of the units of the Division escaped, with untold thousands of enemy troops still bearing down on them.

Behind them, about a half mile south of Kunu-ri, where frozen fields and rice paddies give way to steep rising hills, Baker Company called their march to a halt on the road as two Officers appeared out of the dark to talk to the Baker commander. The unit dropped to the ground for a painful but welcome moments rest.

The commanders' conversation lasted only moments, and ended with the soldiers watching one of the officers' point to a steep mountain nearby. The Baker commander turned and walked slowly back to his men in the darkness. They had drawn the short straw. Company B was assigned as "rear guard" of the rear guard, and would be among the last ones out. They were to take the high ground nearby to cover the Namdae River Bridge that elements of the 38th RCT and other straggler units evacuating still needed to cross. To their rear, south of Kunu-ri, the Division withdrawal was under way. While the 23rd RCT held to protect the Division, Baker Company were to stay behind to protect the backs of their own 23rd Regiment. CPL Chet Thiessen's unit would now be the last unit out, ahead of the onrushing Chinese masses.

For three hours Baker Company dragged their painfully aching bodies and the burden of their weapons and equipment up the near vertical slopes of "Bald Mountain", so named because of the clear lack of trees, brush, or other growth on the summit.

Visibility was good, but the ground was too frozen to dig in, even if the men had the strength left to do so. They scuffed out low spots and rearranged a few rocks and trees to provide cover and fighting positions in a defensive line. Finally, their bodies taking over in self-defense, almost the entire unit passed out in exhaustive sleep.

Out on the flank, in a makeshift, frozen foxhole on "Bald Mountain", after enduring yet another of many long nights under the harsh combat conditions, CPL Thiessen, and PFC's Cartee and Anderson manned their machine gun position. To their front, a clear, open span of white ground spread out before them. Visibility was fairly good, and the team took turns keeping close watch. So far, except for battle noises off in the distance, the bitter cold night had been quiet, and dawn was fast approaching.

"Hey Chet, wake up!" Came a whispered but blunt order from a hoarse and weary voice along with a cautious shake of the other's shoulders. "It's your watch."

Dry, tired and bloodshot eyes opened with a start. CPL Thiessen tried to focus, shaking off the fuzz in his head caused by exhaustion and the cold. In a split second he was alert, the adrenaline rush that seemed to shoot through his system almost continually, again drowning out his bodies scream for rest.

"What!?" He tensed for action, reaching instinctively for his sidearm.

"It's o.k., it's o.k., it's just your watch. So far so good, all quiet on the rice ball front." Anderson answered quietly. "Oh boy, if I can just close my eyes for a few minutes. I hope they don't freeze shut."

"Man, you had to wake me up just now. I was just dreaming about sitting down to a nice ham, mashed potatoes, and some pumpkin pie," Thiessen mumbled with frustration.

"Was there a little whipped cream on the pie?" Asked Anderson.

"Sure was."

"Yeah, you were dreamin' alright. I think I had the same dream the last time I slept, what was it - a week ago?" He mumbled into what became a snore.

Chet took his helmet off and scratched his head furiously for a moment, trying to rearrange his matted hair and get some circulation going to his head, then donned the steel pot again and slid into his familiar position behind the big gun. Anderson was already out like a light. Everything seemed quiet for the moment. With his half-numb trigger finger protruding from a grimy mitten, he carefully rubbed the frost from his eyelashes.

It was in the nearing dawn while he intently watched the open spaces in front of him for signs of the enemy, when he thought he heard a voice whisper what sounded like, "Mano! Mano!" Thinking he may be imagining something, he adjusted his steel pot a little to the side so he could hear better, and racked back the bolt of his machine gun, readying it to fire, just in case.

The whispered words came again, "Mano! Mano!" Before he could think, something flew past his head and landed with a dull thump in the bottom of the frozen hollow spot that served in place of a foxhole. Grenade! Then there was a deafening noise, and everything went black.

Unknown moments later, Thiessen came to; shaking his head to try to clear the ringing in his ears, but the intense pain stopped him from doing so. He was several feet away from the foxhole, where dust and smoke was still settling. Suddenly remembering what had just happened and where he was, he quickly looked around for signs of the enemy, and realized his .30 caliber had followed him in the blast and lay next to him in the snow.

Then he did what every self-respecting American soldier would do. First, after realizing he was sitting out in the open, he got scared, then; realizing what had just happened, he got mad. His head spinning and ears ringing, he quickly cleared the snow and dirt from the machine gun barrel, and bleeding from his eyes, ears, and nose from the effects of the concussion grenade, screamed bloody murder, and fired his heavy machine gun from the hip as he dashed back to his position.

Ignoring the burning pains in his chin, knees, and stomach from grenade shrapnel, he jumped behind the gun tripod sitting awry in the dirt and quickly set the gun in position, and proceeded to shred the enemy soldier who had just thrown the grenade at him into confetti with a devastating blast from his .30 cal. Then, wide eyed and adrenalin pumped, opened up on the screaming mass of enemy soldiers that suddenly appeared out of the darkness and were rushing toward their position.

Though the grenade explosion had blown Chet Thiessen from the hole, it had landed in such a way that it only stunned the others, slamming them harshly against the sides of the shallow fighting position. Flying into action, in spite of the effects of the blast, the other squad members rapidly fed the machine gun and fired their rifles point blank into the onrushing, raging mob.

Quickly assessing the situation, seeing they would soon be overrun, CPL Thiessen ordered his squad, except for Cartee and Anderson manning the gun, to pull back. Seconds later he sent them out too.

"Get the hell out! Pull back!" Screamed CPL Thiessen above the roar of his incessant machine gun blast, "I'm right behind you!"

Cartee and Anderson, bolted away from the rapidly approaching enemy, literally running for their lives with seconds remaining before they were overrun. When they got far enough away to speak, Anderson grabbed Cartee's arm and stopped him.

"Where's Chet?" He panted, gasping for breath.

They both looked at each other questioningly, and then glanced back across the snow covered path they had just travelled. In the distance, over the crest of the mountain top they could still hear the familiar growl of their machine gun firing. Suddenly the machine gun fire stopped. Next, a few small explosions were heard, then nothing. They looked at each other again sadly, and without saying a word, beat a hasty retreat in search of the rest of their unit and the firefight now blazing.

CHAPTER VII

SUICIDE RUN: ESCAPE FROM KUNU-RI

Baker Company fought valiantly against the overwhelming enemy force attempting to drive them from the mountain. When the battle was over, the enemy withdrew, leaving behind as many as 500 of their dead. If the enemy had won out, the fate of the entire 23rd Regiment would have been held in the balance, as the enemy would have had a devastating advantage from the high ground. Baker Company remained on Bald Mountain, watching as thousands upon thousands of Chinese soldiers poured into the valley in the distance, in pursuit of the allied forces. The longer they held, the greater their chances now of being surrounded, a circumstance that would mean certain death.

At last word came. It was time for Baker to gather up their dead and wounded and pull back to join up with the rest of the 23rd. Chet Thiessen's body was not among those carried out.

Finally, the order came to 2nd Division commanders to prepare to evacuate by way of the Kaechon-Sunchon highway, an alternate route that would prevent them from adding to the melee of the southbound rear columns of the 8th Army. The 23rd RCT was ordered to stand and cover the rest of the Divisions withdrawal.

At noon on November 30th, the Division moved out. Though several failed attempts had been made to remove the solid roadblocks manned by the enemy, the plan was to run any roadblocks that stood in the way. The only other option was a suicide stand where they were. While the Division rolled forward in its slow, bumper to bumper exodus on the narrow combat scarred road, the 23rd continued covering the evacuation and fighting off wave after wave of enemy attacks.

On the high ground nearby, "A" battery of the 503rd Field Artillery, covered by the remnants of the 2nd Engineer Combat Battalion, both attached to the 2nd Division, fired their 155mm howitzers point blank into the onrushing Chinese masses, who continued their bloodthirsty rush through storms of exploding flesh and bone. These valiant American soldiers poured out their hellfire until they were finally overrun, giving their lives to the last man.

The "Gauntlet"

Less than a mile down the road, the slow moving columns of trucks, tanks, and men became trapped in a crossfire that rained down from the hills that were controlled by the enemy on both sides of the road. Enemy mortar, machine gun, and small arms fire chewed the units to pieces while exploding and burning trucks hindered the escape route. The wounded held on desperately to the remaining vehicles while the able fired their weapons continuously at the hills above, as our tanks sent their deadly rounds without ceasing until the ammo was gone. It was bitter cold, and when night fell it brought vicious hand to hand combat.

At last, 8,000 meters down the road, what remained of the bumper to bumper convoy escaped the trap, while small groups of soldiers who had taken from the road to whatever cover they could find, made their way out alone to catch up with the Division.

In the rear, the 23rd RCT was still fighting, standing on its own to protect the evacuating Division. With the help of constant air support, fighting with everything they had, the 23rd was holding. When the time came for them to evacuate, the 23rd withdrew and assembled south of Kunu-ri, while the attached tank units provided a curtain of fire from the high ground for protection.

Faced with the prospect of having to take the same escape route as the rest of the Division, the frozen, tired men of the 23rd braced for the onslaught. A message dropped to them from a circling plane gave them new orders – they were to take another way out. The unit would now be evacuating by the Kunu-ri-Sinanju road that as yet appeared to be clear. The orders said move now.

It was hoped that the enemy hadn't made it far enough to give much resistance on this road. However, Baker Company observers from their perch on Bald Mountain had earlier sent repeated reports of enemy troops flowing in that direction. Their chances of success on this route were unknown, and they might also find themselves ripped to shreds in another suicidal gauntlet like the rest of the Division.

Quickly the exhausted and battle weary troops got their column of trucks organized and on the road. The tanks rolled out in the rear, sending salvos of death as going away presents for the enemy.

With darkness upon them, a few miles down the road the 23rd RCT fears were realized and they too, faced an enemy staged gauntlet of their own. The column, congested together, moved steadily along but began taking "burp" gun and other small arms fire from the roadsides. The troops riding on tanks and in open trucks were sitting ducks. Whenever the column slowed, the vehicles were mobbed by enemy masses in the dark that tried to pull the men from the vehicles.

Men wounded by enemy gunfire, who could not be grabbed in time, toppled from the vehicles and had to be left behind, because the column could not stop. Literal "tug of war" evolved all along the column as the enemy struggled to pull men from the vehicles, while the men of the 23rd held on. It was impossible to see enemy targets in the dark to effectively defend themselves from the moving column. Baker Company had lost another dozen men that night before clearing the enemy forces.

In the last five days, the 2nd Division had suffered nearly 4,700 casualties, but they had made the enemy pay dearly for every single one.

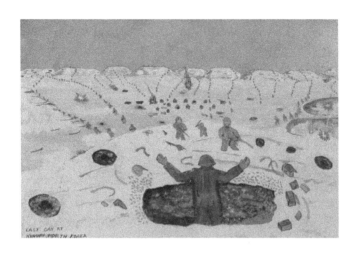

CHAPTER VIII

PRISONER OF WAR

After Cartee and Anderson had fled their machine gun position and joined up with the rest of their unit, CPL Chet Thiessen had every intention of joining them, but the enemy was advancing on his position so fast he couldn't stop firing long enough to bail out.

The glowing red hot barrel of his air cooled machine gun seemed to sag under its own weight as it belched forth round upon round of searing lead into the onrushing enemy. He didn't even need to pull the trigger anymore, because the breech[1] was so hot the gunpowder in the shells was igniting on its own. All he had to do was aim and keep the ammo belts coming. A continuous rain of brass shells sprang from the ejection port of the machine gun and covered the bottom of the foxhole. There was no time to appreciate the fleeting warmth of the hot brass, while the frozen earth all around him seemed alive as it churned and leapt into the air in stinging gusts as the enemy bullets reached out to tear at everything around him. All the fire of the enemy onslaught before him was concentrated on silencing him and his weapon.

Suddenly, as the last ammo belt came to an end, the machine gun fell silent. His hand instinctively fell to his sidearm, and he sent his last 10 rounds as fast as possible downrange. Scrambling, CPL Thiessen tore at the pockets of his field jacket and found the four grenades he carried. Pulling the pins one by one, he threw them as fast and as effectively he could at the closely advancing enemy.

"I was all out of any kind of ammo. About the only thing left I had to defend myself with was bad words.

---

[1] The breech is the chamber where the bullet or shell is inserted to fire. Continuous firing of an automatic weapon can get it so hot the gunpowder in the bullets ignites on their own and the gun can actually fire by itself. The only thing that stops it is to run it out of ammo. This is a condition the military calls "cook-off".

Several enemy soldiers moved up on me. They stopped firing, and I grabbed on to my e-tool[2] and threw that at one of them. They walked right up to me with guns pointed. I thought it was all over. I don't know why they didn't kill me. I still wonder about that to this day.

From behind the group of soldiers, a Chinese officer walked up towards me. Remembering the knife I had stashed in my boot, I quickly grabbed the knife and threw it at him but he ducked it, and I missed. That was all I had. I stood there defiantly waiting for him to order his men to kill me, and he never said anything, just sort of smiled and waved at me to come forward. At the end of several gun barrels I followed him. I looked at the scene as we walked past, and I silently took consolation from the nice big pile of dead Chinese bodies that lay in front of my machine gun position. I was taken prisoner, but look what it took for them to take me - and <u>only</u> because I was out of ammo!"

The next weeks found CPL Thiessen being bound, beaten, and marched from place to place. The first days he remembers, but the conditions he was to endure after that were hazy at best.

---

[2] E-tool is military jargon for the "Entrenching tool" or small folding shovel/axe carried by soldiers.

"*I was starving, marched from camp to camp, and shoved into bunker after bunker. When they finally gave me some food for the first time, it was only a ball of rice. Then they pissed on the rice and laughed at me. I refused to eat it. But after four days of not eating and staring at it I finally had to give in. I guess at some point between starvation, cold, and captivity I stopped feeling too much of anything about anything. I refuse to eat rice to this day.*"

Day after day, the 18 year old Corporal endured multiple beatings, compounding the concussion and what appeared to be broken ribs he had already suffered from the grenade blast. The obstinace and tenacity he had developed as a kid on the streets of Grand Rapids, came back to haunt, and protect him, potentially saving his life.

"It seemed like every day, about every hour or two, four or five of the gooks would come in the bunker where I was held, and then it would start. They would kick me and beat me over and over. I was only a Corporal and couldn't understand a word they said, so the only thing I could think of is that it entertained them. It certainly wasn't any type of interrogation.

I was pathetically weak from starvation; they would constantly piss in my filth ridden rice and my drinking water. In defiance, I resisted eating or drinking all I could. They beat me all day long, and marched me all night as well, and if I didn't keep up, they'd kick me some more. But with every bit of strength I could muster, I gave it right back to them. If I could get my hands or feet free in any way, I would fight back, punching, scratching, kicking, and screaming. I decided the only way those devils would ever get the best of me is if they killed me.

I really don't remember much more than that after the first week. What I do remember though, is that pretty much pure hatred of the enemy drove me. My wounds, the beatings, starvation, dehydration, sub-zero weather,[3] constant night marches moving from place to place, and regular napalm drops and strafing from friendly air

---

[3] According to the 23rd Infantry "Secret" Command Report for December 1951, cold weather clothing was not issued to the soldiers until sometime in December during the re-build effort following the devastating 8th Army withdrawal from the North. Corporal Thiessen therefore would have had to endure his entire captivity without any winter clothing.

strikes while in enemy hands, took their toll on me. After a few days it all became a staggering blur and I lost all track of time. Soon I began to consider myself basically already dead, but resolved that if they wanted my life, they would have to take it, because I wasn't going to give it up willingly. Not today, not tomorrow, not to them. Defiance of my captors became my only emotion and purpose.

All the while he was captive; CPL Thiessen thought he was being marched to the north, where he had heard there were prison camps. Fortunately he had been marched southward toward friendly lines where the enemy was massing for its next offensives against allied forces. A chance Marine Corps raid on an enemy camp one day changed everything.

"Finally, I was stuck in yet another stinking bunker somewhere, and the enemy camp got hit and taken over by our Marines. I was startled to hear people speaking English! I was so afraid after all I'd been through our guys would shoot me by mistake. I had to call out that I was an American.

I had given up hope of ever being free, but by a stroke of fateful luck, I was liberated that day."

The Marines were able to get Chet Thiessen back near his unit, but they were unable to take him all the way there. The Marines had no supplies or weapons to spare, so CPL Thiessen, still in the delirium suffered from the effects of his captivity, had to struggle to make his way, alone and unarmed, a mile or more through enemy territory until he found the 23rd RCT on a ridge in front of him. CPL Thiessen carefully made his way toward the line, finally calling out to the sentries so they wouldn't shoot him.

"Hey, don't shoot!"

"Who are you?" Came a voice from behind a log bunker.

"CPL Chet Thiessen, Baker Company."

"What the heck are you doin' out there?"

"I've been a P.O.W. The Marines just found me and sent me here."

"Come on in soldier."

As quickly as his weak body allowed, CPL Thiessen scrambled up the hill, where he was greeted by friendly troops. He was sent to the Sargent in charge.

"Where you been Corporal?"

"I've been a P.O.W. Sarge. The Marines raided the camp where I was being held." The weary Corporal explained.

"How long?"

The young soldier tried to think through the fuzzy haze in his head. "I – I think maybe a week or two, I think. What day is it anyway?"

Chet Thiessen would find to his surprise that five weeks had passed since his capture by the Chinese. There was no debriefing, no fanfare. The

Sargent sent him to their supply where he could draw another .30 Caliber machine gun, then to the mess tent where he could find some chow.

Completely exhausted after his ordeal as a prisoner, he had marched for a full day and a half with the Marine unit before being repatriated. Functioning on less than two hours sleep over the previous two days, he dutifully went and drew another weapon first, and then, in his great hunger, went to the mess tent to finally get some desperately needed food.

"I went to the mess tent and got some food. I was so happy I could finally sit down and rest for a minute and eat a hot meal. I don't think I had eaten more than one bite, I know I hadn't swallowed it yet when the mess sergeant told me to pack it up, we were moving out for a place called the 'twin tunnels'. They took my food from me and sent me to a supply tent where I could find some cold rations. I went to the supply tent and found the rations. I was so tired and so hungry I could hardly move, but I picked through the boxes and found my favorite. Some kind of sausage, and an orange candy thing. I got several cans out and tried to heat them up over a little 'canned heat' burner right there in the tent. It tasted so good. I think I had been back less than an hour, and then we were moving out."

Any debriefing or hopes of rest or medical attention for the weary soldier was not to be. The 2nd Division was back on the march again. Ahead lay the test for the UN forces. Could they defeat the overwhelming numbers of the Communist armies, or should they cut their losses and relinquish South Korea to them? The coming weeks would tell.

CHAPTER IX

RIGHT BACK IN THE SADDLE

Due to our mobilization capabilities, the 8th Army units were able in a short time to outrun the foot borne CCF troops that had inflicted such devastating losses in lives and equipment only days before. The 8th Army soon found itself south of the 38th Parallel back in southern Korea territory. The X Corps troops that had been fighting on the eastern section of the allied lines when the Chinese hit in full fury had faced a similar devastation as it withdrew from the Cho-sin Reservoir and across the mountains to the port of Hungnam where the U.S. Navy was waiting to evacuate the X Corps by sea.

The Chinese forces didn't have the mobility or logistics to match the UN forces, and this allowed allied troops to rest and re-equip, though spending most of their time in the outdoors of nature's own merciless and punishing winter sub-zero weather, in order to regroup to meet the unknown intentions of the slowly but certainly approaching Chinese Communist Forces. It was not yet known if China was satisfied with driving the allied forces south of the parallel, and would cease their advance.

Battalions from Greece, France, Netherlands, Belgium, and Brazil now joined the American regiments, with the French becoming as a fourth Battalion of the 23rd RCT. Once the X Corps had recovered from their amphibious evacuation at Hungnam, they joined the 8th Army, bringing along their Marine Corps Division (to the many thanks of CPL Thiessen, and the chagrin of his captors). New arms and equipment continued to arrive.

The question of the CCF intent was soon known after their supply lines caught up with their troops and thousands of Chinese and North Korean forces crossed the 38th Parallel in its third offensive on 1 January 1951. The war had returned. The 23rd RCT was now officially back in battle, amidst heavy combat, eliminating a roadblock near Hoengsong, about 10 miles north of Wonju, on 2 January, and dug in in defensive positions there, amidst 20 below zero temperatures, until January 5th, when, according to what limited information he was able to obtain when battered and weary former P.O.W. Chet Thiessen was repatriated to his unit, is approximately the day he rejoined the war.

Why Wonju?

The few main roads that existed in Korea were imperative to both sides for moving ammo, supplies, and equipment. Towns that contained several main road junctions were critical to the allied forces to both restrict enemy avenues of approach to the south and provide movement of friendly forces to the north. The southern Korean town of Wonju was just one of those places. Five major road thoroughfares passed through Wonju as well as it serving as a railroad junction. On 6 January, 10,000 enemy troops moved toward the allied defenses arrayed between Wonju and Chechon, several mile south of the 23rd's defensive positions.

New orders came. The 23rd were to immediately pull back to Wonju, and ordered to blow all the bridges on the way as they cleared them to hinder further enemy advances. By 1500 hours, the 23rd and 38th Regiments began moving in to secure the best defensive terrain around the town of Wonju. If Wonju fell, it would leave the Communist forces poised for a drive to Pusan, possibly driving the allied forces from Korea and into the ocean at their backs.

Wonju falls

On 7 January, three North Korean Divisions, along with unknown amounts of Chinese forces slammed hard against the Wonju defenders, while another entire North Korean Division was moving fast out of the north on the road from Hoengsong to reinforce the battle.

The battle for Wonju raged on and on all night long. Finally an allied ammunition train staged in Wonju was blown by allied forces and the railroad bridge, after a demolition charge failed to explode, was set afire with gasoline to destroy it. Soon the defenders were driven from the town to new defensive positions on the high ground south of town. Near Chupori, protecting the main road leading south out of Wonju, the 9th RCT was dealing with an enemy regiment attempting to cut off the 2nd Division's escape route to points south.

Orders came from X Corps command that Wonju must be retaken. Assaults to do so were repelled after bitter fighting on 8 January. Another attempt, on 9 January also failed. The combat raged in subzero weather conditions that mirrored that of the November warfare at Kunu-ri.

In the early hours of 10 January, large groups of enemy forces moved out from Wonju to attack 2nd Division positions, and were spotted by aerial observation planes. Friendly fire was poured down on the attacking enemy troops, taking heavy casualties and soon sending them on the run. After several more days of incessant fighting, the important town of Wonju fell again to allied control as the enemy silently withdrew from the town.

Patrolling commenced, searching out the enemy. Little contact was made and friendly forces found Hoengsong, ten mile to the north, free of enemy troops. In the following days, patrols made more and more contact with enemy units in the area, and some were found digging in north of Hoengsong. Orders were issued to continually send seek and destroy patrols out to keep the area swept of any massing of enemy forces.

"Twin Tunnels"

Historians and military strategists have dubbed the action west of Wonju and southeast of Chipyong-ni that of the "twin tunnels", which were actually two railroad tunnels not far apart from each other.

On 28 January a Baker Company patrol discovered enemy troops in the twin tunnels area. A larger force was sent out to deal with the enemy in the area and later found themselves surrounded. Air drops were required to resupply the patrol as another Company fought their way through in close combat to provide them a way out.

Two Battalions of the 23rd Regiment swept down on the twin tunnels area on 31 January, supported by the 37th Field Artillery. CPL Chet Thiessen moved with his machine gun team with Baker Company from the 1st Battalion base at Iho-ri, just south of Wonju to provide a defensive perimeter of infantry around the positions of the 37th Field Artillery unit.

The 23rd RCT offensive was successful and a defensive perimeter was established. At 0450 hours on 1 February the 23rd positions were slammed by two enemy regiments. Amidst the shrill warning cries of bugles and whistles the Chinese hordes raged against the defenders, who soon had to call for reinforcements. The 1st Battalion immediately responded from its base at Iho-ri, charging to the aid of its fellow Battalions. Elsewhere CPL Thiessen was busy with the rest of Baker Company whose positions had been penetrated by masses of enemy troops attempting to take out the guns of the 37th Field. Baker successfully provided close-in defensive fighting while the artillery continued to fire non-stop in their support of the fray engaged in by the three Battalions of the 23rd RCT, as large groups of enemy troops tried to encircle both flanks.

When the battle ended, the enemy had withdrawn leaving 3600 enemy causalities behind; 1300 enemy dead lay in front of the 23rd RCT positions.

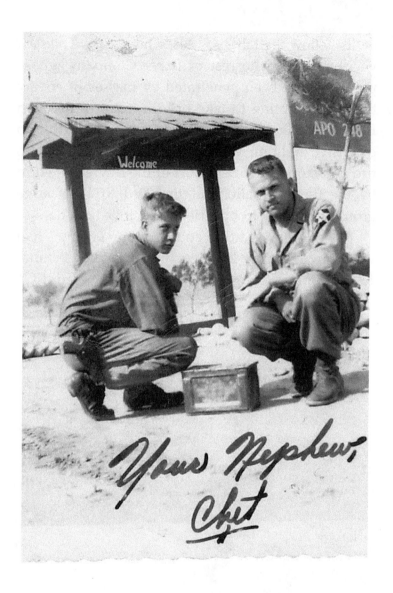

Chet Thiessen (left) with another Grand Rapids, Michigan soldier in Korea 1951

CHAPTER X

FIGHTING A WAR IN KOREA

Continuous patrolling by allied forces was imperative to keep tabs on the enemy and keep the areas friendly forces held secure. CPL Thiessen seemed to develop a type of popularity when it came to leading these patrols.

"Today I still shake my head at how things went for me sometimes on the line. It didn't matter what we had been through that day, but it seemed like when it came time that someone decided to send a patrol out, someone (I never really knew who ordered it) way down the line would call for 'Thiessen' to gather some men and lead a patrol somewhere seeking out enemy troops. It would get whispered all down the line, passed from foxhole to foxhole until it finally came to me. I would get some guys, find out where we were supposed go, and head out. I must have had sucker marked on my forehead or something," joked Chet.

S.I.W. – self-inflicted wounds

"One day we were on patrol near a railroad track. A train was heading south toward our lines, and we hadn't had any word to expect any traffic out of the north, so we set up a blocking type ambush and stopped the train on the tracks. We carefully boarded the train and found it full of what appeared to be allied wounded. Not knowing what was going on, and fearing an enemy trick, since everyone on the train appeared to be American and we knew the North Korean's were armed and trained by the Russian's, we held the officer in charge with a gun to his head. All the wounded were tagged with tags marked 'S.I.W.' Demanding to know where they were going, he explained that these men had all shot themselves in the feet or hands – self-inflicted wounds - to get out of fighting."

"Once we were satisfied they were friendly forces, we let them go. Our whole patrol was very angry at what we had found. There were a lot of guys on the line – almost every one – that didn't want to be here fighting, but they stayed and did their job. One less man on the line put everyone at risk, plus, other men had to pull off the line to help the S.I.W. back to an aid station. It was a sad and dangerous situation."

Enemy Snipers

One of the risks of being a combat leader is that of being a primary target for the enemy. The idea being that if the leader is killed, the troops won't know what to do. In Korea, snipers were always a threat, especially to our officers and senior NCO's.[4]

---

[4] NCO is abbreviation for "non-commissioned officer". Applies to ranks of Corporal and all Sergeants, technically all military leaders who do not receive an officers "commission".

"One day, I don't remember exactly where we were at, but we were all dug in on another ridge somewhere, and for some reason we had a new Captain on the line. He had just come in from the rear, all spit shined boots, with a clean, crisp uniform, and strutting about like a General, bluntly barking orders at everyone. We had been in combat for several days, and were unshaven, exhausted, dirty, cold, and he walked up to us in our foxhole and demanded gruffly that we get ourselves shaved and washed up. There was no water, and the enemy could attack at any minute. Seeing his gleaming brass bars on his helmet and knowing the danger to him from snipers all around us, the only answer I gave him was, "Sir, you better get those #@%& bars off your helmet before you get killed. There's snipers out here!"

Well that just made him mad. He told me bluntly that if I talked to him like that again he would have me court-martialed. I thanked him somewhat sarcastically, with all due respect, that at least it would get me the hell off the line for a while. He was a little taken back and seemed to think about that for a second, then not so politely told us that all we had to worry about was following orders, and the next time he saw us we should be clean shaven. I don't think it was twenty minutes and he fell dead nearby, with an enemy sniper bullet hole right through his Captains bars on the front of his helmet. Experienced combat officers already knew that shiny brass made a perfect target for snipers even a mile or more away."

Safer in the foxhole?

"I remember one night that Roy, Bernie, and I were somewhere out on the line in a hole. It was colder than Billy hell. I had to make my way up to the mess tent to get rations. Inside there were boxes and boxes of mortar shells and other ammunition in crates stacked all around. From what I could see was going on, there was a group of officers who decided that they wanted to sleep where it was warm instead of out in some frozen bunker like the rest of the troops and had pulled all of the empty stretchers out of the ambulances and laid them like bunks across the ammo boxes.

Later on that night, an enemy mortar barrage started to come in. The Chinese were very good with their mortars and I don't think they walked in four rounds before they laid a direct hit on the mess hall with all those officers stretched out on top of crates upon crates of high explosive mortar rounds. The only thing left was a big crater."

Teatime for the fighting Brits'

"At one point in time we were fighting alongside the British troops. While we were marching forward to what was the front line area, one group of Brit's were marching the opposite direction. One of the guys at the head of the line was wearing a Scottish kilt and playing the bagpipes as they marched along. It was quite a sound against the battle noise in the near distance.

After reaching the front line, we started taking enemy mortar fire and had to quickly take cover. Not far from our new position, I could see some other British troops nearby. I couldn't believe what I was seeing. While we were running for cover in the middle of this barrage, I could see the Brits sitting calmly in their foxholes enjoying their tea and biscuits! Not even a Chinese mortar barrage was going to interrupt their 'tea time'."

Feet dry: practical ingenuity

"One problem we had almost continually was wet socks. It was so important to keep our feet dry, but nearly impossible because of both sweating and the snow. One trick we learned was to change our socks every chance we had, and tuck the damp socks into the armpit area of our field jackets. Our body heat would slowly dry the socks out so we could have dry socks from time to time."

Hunger in the foxhole

It is a well-known axiom in the military that an army can fight without food or water, but an army cannot fight without ammunition. Thus, on the list of priorities for military supply efforts, ammunition is always on the top. The desperate re-supply effort at Chipyong-ni and elsewhere was no different, making rations (and the time to eat them) often very scarce.

"I remember Bernie, Roy, and I and a couple other guys were on watch, and we were starving. One of them shot a seagull that was flying over nearby and it fell from

the sky right next to us. We tore that seagull apart and ate it raw. You have to be pretty hungry to do that. The only part that made everyone mad was that once you get past the feathers, there isn't much to a seagull, and we were still hungry."

The challenge of winter combat

The month of November in 1950 brought with it winter, and sub-zero temperatures that introduced a different kind of enemy onto the battlefield that threatened the lives of the soldiers of both sides. The freezing temperatures found many of our soldiers ill equipped to face the weather . All winter gear available was issued to the front line troops, but there wasn't nearly enough for all the men. Chet Thiessen remembers that the freezing temperatures endured on the battlefield were often possibly a greater threat than even enemy bullets:

"On a few rare occasions when I was able to leave my machine gun position for a few minutes, I had opportunity to help evacuate the wounded off the line and back to the medics nearby. I was surprised to learn that most of the wounded had little chance of survival, and even what would normally be considered minor flesh wounds were often fatal because the subzero temperatures made the effects of normal shock that came with being wounded far more devastating."

Deadly cold

The frozen battlefield conditions weren't just a danger to the mortality of the wounded, but even dealt fatal blows of its own:

"We had been in combat for some time, and had lost a lot of men. Our replacement troops later became Army Reservists and National Guardsmen. As I understand things these guys were brought in as fast as possible, and probably didn't have a chance to prepare for the weather and other conditions we were facing. I had a new guy in my squad – he wasn't with us long enough for me to even get a chance to know his name – but even though I did everything I could to keep him awake and moving, even reaching over several times with my foot to kick him to keep him from falling asleep, while at the same time manning my machine gun, but he apparently finally gave in to the cold. When the sun came up the next morning we found he had frozen to death. His body had frozen solid during the night."

Frostbite and frozen limbs

Shortages of winter gear, harsh terrain, and lack of accessible routes of transportation made it difficult to equip our soldiers with everything they needed to fight such a difficult war in such difficult weather conditions:

"In the winter we were issued what we called "shoepacks". These were basically a rubber shoe cover

with leather leggings of some sort. There wasn't any kind of insulation to them at all.

At one point I had to give in and seek medical attention at an aid station a few miles back from our position. My feet and lower legs had lost all feeling and appeared to me to have nearly frozen solid. I was miserable and hobbled stiff legged through the snow to the aid station to find out that I had received severe frostbite to both feet and lower legs. The Doctor who examined me was concerned and scheduled me for immediate surgery to amputate both of my legs below the knee.

I very impolitely objected, actually calling the Doctor a lot of things I can't repeat, and he conceded by giving me some purple stuff he told me to paint my legs and feet with, and I struggled to walk back to the front line. Though I have had to suffer with the effects of the frost bite the rest of my life on my face, hands, legs and feet, somehow between the purple medication and my walk back to the front, my feet were able to thaw, and I was able to save my legs."

Breakfast on the Han (at -30 below)

The heroic efforts of the soldiers didn't always have to come from firing a weapon. Others did all they could to support the beleaguered troops that stood against both enemy and nature:

"One day we got word that somebody in the Mess decided that they were going to do all they could to get us

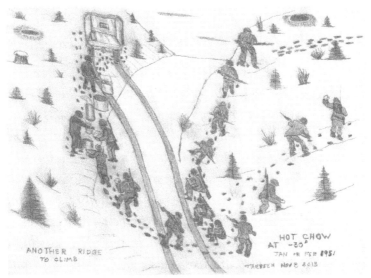

a hot meal on the front. It sometimes went down to 40 below out there. I remember they were calling us a few at a time to pull off the line and move down to where the makeshift Mess had set up. When I got there, the steam was everywhere, like clouds, coming from the heated pots.

I was so excited to get a hot meal, and when I saw all that food cooking I couldn't wait to get some. We had to cross a road, which was only really about twenty feet wide, to where the field kitchen was setting. There was this huge pot of steaming hot scrambled eggs. I got a mess kit full of those eggs, and whatever else they had there, and couldn't wait to dig in. I hurried back across the road and quickly sat down on a rock. I took my spoon to dig in to those beautiful hot eggs, and in those few seconds it took me to cross the road, found they had already frozen solid. I chopped them up and ate them anyway! Boy how we appreciated what those guys had tried to do for us."

Without a trace

"All of our machine gun ammo belts included tracer rounds. We had a heck of a time with the canvass belts, because each of the tracers had to be pulled from the belt before we could use them, and the bullet casings weren't exactly smooth like todays ammo, and that, combined with a little frost made it so we had to actually twist them out of the straps holding them in the belt. Tracers work great to help a machine gun sight in on a long distance target, but they also are like a laser beam pointing right back at your position, giving the enemy mortars what they are looking for – a target!

Standing Against Chinese "Human Wave" Attacks

Chet Thiessen explains what it was like fighting against the massive enemy human wave type attacks:

"The only way to describe what it was like fighting against the human wave attacks of the Chinese, and in some cases the North Koreans, is that though we fought with all we had, there were just so many of them! Firing as fast as we could, it was impossible to kill them fast enough to stop them. The dead enemy bodies would be piled sometimes - and I don't think I would be exaggerating if I were to say several feet high - in front of our position, and no matter how many we mowed down,

more of those screaming Reds just kept coming at us over the top of the pile. Then they'd overrun the line and we had to face them hand to hand, or literally dig them out our foxholes with fixed bayonet's. I don't think anyone could really appreciate what this was like unless they were there. So many times my air-cooled machine gun barrel would be glowing red hot, and almost seemed to visibly sag or bend slightly under its own weight. It was incredible."

Cartee

"Bernie was a remarkable combat soldier. He was incredibly strong. I personally saw him snap an enemy soldiers arm with one hand once when we were fighting in a hand-to-hand situation. He was also very good with a knife and naturally stealthy. Every once in a while, he must have gotten bored or something on night watch, and *he would strip off his gear, grab just his knife, and tell me he would be back in a while. He would slip out of our foxhole and head out toward enemy lines in the pitch dark. He would be gone for a couple hours, then he would slip right back into our foxhole before we knew he was even there, normally covered with blood - but not his."*

Bernie Cartee
Korea, summer 1951

A miracle on the battlefield?

"I don't remember where it was at now, but there was a M.A.S.H. Hospital set up in a valley area. We fought a battle all day long all around it, and the ground it was on changed hands three times between us and the enemy that day. After it was all over, not a single person in that tent hospital was injured, not a doctor, nurse, or wounded.

Above: Winter patrols in knee deep snow and freezing temperatures

Below: Winter combat in the open; no cover

Above: Base Camp stand down, summer 1951

Below: Korean children hanging around base camp; in spite of the ravages of war, kids always manage to find time to play.

Mama san took care of the soldiers base camp laundry

Chet sharing a light hearted moment with a South Korean houseboy during a rare respite from combat

Chet posing by helicopter used to carry wounded out of combat

117

French soldiers attached to the 23rd RCT

Fellow American soldiers of the 23rd RCT

A good example of the terrain challenges of the northern Korean countryside

Inje Valley

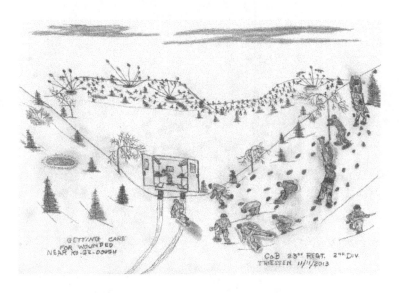

CHAPTER XI

A BATTLEFIELD COMMISSION

One frigid morning, CPL Thiessen could hear his name being passed down the line as usual. Thinking it was time for him to lead another patrol out; he was surprised to be informed that there was a jeep waiting to take him back to Regimental Headquarters. Carefully, he pulled back from his fighting position and slowly made his way to where the jeep was waiting.

After a bumpy ride back to Regiment, the jeep pulled up in front of the Command tent where there was already a line of soldiers waiting to enter. CPL Thiessen wandered over and got in line with the rest, still wondering what the whole to-do was all about. When he entered the tent, he was met by the First Sergeant[5] who held a clipboard in his hands.

---

[5] The "First Sergeant" is the highest ranking NCO in a typically Company sized military unit. The First Sergeant, also affectionately and respectfully referred to as "Top" is typically

"Name?" Demanded the First Sergeant.

"Thiessen, Chester G., Corporal, First Sergeant."

"Baker Company?"

"Yes First Sergeant." Replied the wondering Corporal.

"Be sure you remember to give Freeman the high-ball."[6]

"Yes First Sergeant." Now really wondering what Colonel Freeman, the 23rd Regimental Commander would want of him, especially after sending up a jeep and a driver.

The young Corporal soon stood before the Regimental Commander, who was seated behind a table that held a stack of files. He snapped to attention before the Colonel and gave his best salute.

"Corporal Thiessen reporting as ordered sir."

"Thiessen, would you accept a battlefield commission as a Second Lieutenant?" Inquired the Regimental Commander firmly.

Taken off guard, the young soldier mulled a lot of thoughts over in a matter of seconds. It was quite a compliment to the 18 year old that someone

---

a Master Sergeant specifically identified with an additional diamond shape set inside the opening inside the stripes, unless they are a Sergeant Major who is designated by a star instead of a diamond.

[6] A salute in this case was something that all had to be reminded to do, as soldiers don't typically salute in the field because the enemy can easily identify the officers by who is saluted. Soldiers also rarely ever salute when they are armed.

thought he had the leadership skills to be an officer and assume command of a platoon, however, hard combat experience compelled him to give the only answer that made any sense at the time.

"No sir!"

"Why?" The Colonel demanded.

"Sir, I think I can survive this war and make it home as a Corporal, I'm not so sure I'll be able to do that as a Lieutenant."

The Commander smiled slightly and nodded, as if he appreciated the answer. The two exchanged salutes and the jeep driver dutifully returned CPL Thiessen to the front and back to his familiar place in the cold foxhole behind his machine gun.

Upon his return, Chet Thiessen's patrol leading duties continued, and even seemed to intensify.

"I swear the only word they knew that came after 'patrol' was 'Chet'!"

About two weeks later, the familiar name came ringing down the line again. He was told that there was a jeep waiting to take him back to Regimental Command. Again, he cautiously pulled off the line and made his way to the waiting jeep, manned this time with a different driver, who again drove him over war ravaged hill and dale to the Regimental Command tent, just like when he was there a couple weeks before.

Not quite sure what this was about this time, CPL Thiessen joined the line and waited his turn to enter the command tent. When he finally entered, there stood the same First Sergeant, in the same spot, with the same clipboard.

"Name?" Barked the First Sergeant.

"Thiessen, Chester G., Corporal, First Sergeant."

"Baker Company?"

"Yes First Sergeant." Now CPL Thiessen really wondered what was going on.

"Be sure you remember to give Freeman the high-ball."

"Yes First Sergeant."

In an incredulous replay of previous events, the young Corporal found himself again at attention before the Regimental Commander.

"Corporal Thiessen reporting as ordered sir."

The Colonel looked up at him questioningly as if he remembered him from before. Then asked the same question he had the last time he was here.

"Thiessen, would you accept a battlefield commission as a Second Lieutenant?"

"No sir!" He responded the same as before.

"Why?" Came the same question back.

"Sir, I think I can survive this war and make it home as a Corporal, I'm not so sure I'll be able to do that as a Lieutenant." Answered Chet Thiessen, exactly the same as he had during the previous encounter, this time with even more conviction.

Colonel Freeman gave him a puzzled look, then burst out heartily laughing, finally waving CPL Thiessen away with a smile.

"The Colonel laughed so hard I thought he was going to fall off his chair!" Recollected Chet. *"If I remember right, he was still laughing when I left the command tent. I never got asked again. I've always wondered if after that maybe he thought I was too smart to be a Lieutenant."*

CHAPTER XII

DIGGING IN AT CHIPYONG-NI

With the conclusion of the brutal fighting at the "Twin Tunnels", intelligence reports were showing a massive increase in enemy build-up near the town of Wonju, and in the area of Chipyong-ni to the northwest. Like Wonju, the small village of

Chipyong-ni also held critical road junctions and railroad access.

On 3 February the 23rd RCT moved in to secure Chipyong-ni with little enemy resistance. By nightfall, the town was theirs. Unlike most war torn villages and towns in central Korea, Chipyong-ni was in relatively good condition. Sitting amidst a small valley surrounded by low lying hills, many civilians still lived in houses in the village. Near the outside of the town were several frozen rice paddies and farm fields, and out in the distance many higher hills loomed. Five key roads came together here, as well as the railroad that passed over the road leading there from the south from the Twin Tunnels area.

The Regimental Command was set up in a school, with the 1st Battalion Command nearby. Though high ground in the distance would have been more advantageous to occupy, there weren't enough troops to go around, so Col. Freeman, the Regimental commander deployed his troops in a circular perimeter defense around the town on the ring of low lying hills. To the north, units of the 1st Battalion dug in, to the west, the 3rd Battalion, on the south edge the 2nd Battalion, and at the eastern section of the circle, units of the attached French Battalion. On the frozen fields and rice paddies, the gun crews of the 37th and 503rd Field Artillery set-up shop, while many attached tank units spread about to provide mobile firepower where needed. Mortar units arrayed their lethal barrels about the inside of the perimeter. Baker Company, along with the recently attached 1st Ranger Company, were designated the Regimental reserve force. At the same time, Baker Company, with Chet Thiessen, Bernie Cartee, and Roy Anderson in their ranks was assigned daily patrolling duties in every direction, in search of enemy units.

Elsewhere, other units of the 2nd Division were setting up defensive lines as well. The 9th RCT, some miles distant, was to the right of the 23rd, and beyond that, near Hoengsong, was 38th RCT. A new offensive was being planned, and Division forces were to act in support of several attacking ROK units. Incessant patrols by Baker Company and other Division units began making more and more contact with small enemy groups. The frequency of enemy probing attacks against friendly positions began to increase in frequency, giving evidence of another possible major enemy offensive.

The weather conditions caused many difficulties. Patrols and supply transport faced thawing days and freezing nights that made the roads either masses of mud or rough, hard frozen ruts. Air cover was hindered by bad weather as well. Evidence was pointing to a substantial enemy build up in the Wonju region, and in the areas east, near Chipyong-ni.

In spite of the challenges pressed by weather, the 23rd RCT at Chipyong-ni continued digging in and hardening their positions. Soldiers fighting positions were dug deeper and reinforced. Barbed wire was strung at strategic positions around the perimeter. Trip flares and anti-personnel mines were installed forward of the positions. Ranges were dialed in, and fields of fire were marked out. Ammunition was distributed and stockpiled in the foxholes. An impenetrable defensive perimeter was being established. The 23rd was digging in solid, and planning for an extended stay.

Outpost on Hill 506

The increase of enemy concentration in the area around Chipyong-ni made commanders concerned about an enemy advantage from nearby Hill 506, closest to the regimental perimeter. On 9 February, Chet Thiessen marched with Baker Company through the 3rd Battalion line and outside the defensive perimeter toward the distant, snow covered height of Hill 506.

As they passed through the lines, L Company soldiers of the 3rd Battalion razzed the Baker Company troops.

"Hey, aren't you guys going to stay around for the fun, or are you off for some R & R in Japan?"[7]

---

[7] Rest & Relaxation.

Bernie Cartee, piped back, "I'm feeling mighty charitable today bud, I'll gladly let you take my place on this trip!"

Nobody volunteered.

The soldiers of Baker Company trudged forward bravely to accomplish their mission – secure Hill 506 and deny its use to the enemy. Everyone knew that a major enemy offensive may be in the works, and it was with trepidation Baker Company began their ascent of Hill 506 slogging through knee deep snow. Every man knew that it was very possible being so far away from the support of the rest of the regiment, that Baker could easily get surrounded and cut off. And, if that happened, every man also knew, more than likely, Baker Company wouldn't be coming back.

Under the burden of the weight of the machine gun, ammo, rations, and other needed supplies, Chet Thiessen and his squad struggled forward up the nearly vertical slope. The underbrush was so thick it was nearly impassible in good weather, let alone buried in a couple feet of snow.

"Hey Chet," Cartee whispered, gasping for breath as he stomped a branch down out of his way so he could step over, "If the gooks are here, how would we know? They could be standing right next to us and we couldn't see them!"

"Heck, if we do find any, they'll be close enough to shake hands with by the time we see each other."

Thiessen panted. "I just hope we get to the top of this damn hill before dark, or we'll really be in the soup."

"Man!" Quipped Roy Anderson, "Soup sounds good right now, especially if it isn't frozen solid. I never thought I'd see the day that I had to cut my food with a hammer. How much farther?"

"Can't tell. But the sun is goin' down fast and isn't going to wait for us, that's for sure," replied Thiessen. "We better keep pushing. We still have to set up our positions when we get to the top. If it's even possible in this thicket! By the way, is that all you think about is food?"

"Heck no!" Anderson shot back, "But I ain't seen a woman in so long I forgot what they look like. So I think about food."

"I wished that worked for me," Cartee piped in, wrestling to adjust his pack straps on his shoulders. "The stuff they try to pass off around here as food reminds me of women even more."

"It does? Why?" Inquired Anderson curiously, stopping to rub his eye where a branch had scratched his face.

"Because most of the time it doesn't agree with me either!"

Amidst quiet, knowing chuckles, the battle hardened but weary young men plodded upward.

As the sun settled in the west, Baker Company crested the hill and hastily set up their defenses. No enemy contact had been made so far, but if command had seen the advantage of this height, the enemy commanders saw the same advantage. The chance of unfriendly company coming to call was great. The unit quickly deployed, in practiced efficiency, scuffing out fighting positions as best they could in the frozen environment, and knocking down what brush they could so they could at least have some visibility. As another anxious Korean night fell, the men shivered in the bitter cold darkness, crouched in their fighting positions, keenly aware that they were in a very vulnerable situation, thinking of home and pondering what the days ahead would bring.

The endless night turned slowly into daylight. That night and next day saw no enemy contact and allowed the men of Baker Company to improve their positions as best they could, and gave them the chance to at least move around to stay warm, a luxury not granted during the coldest time at night. Visibility for the most part, because of the thicket, was extremely limited. A second night fell on the lonely outpost.

Just before dawn, the enemy stumbled upon the outpost. After a brief but furious exchange, the enemy withdrew. Every indication was that the enemy didn't expect to find them there. The after action found several enemy dead littering the snow outside their defenses. Two Baker Company troops though, were dead as well, and three wounded.

A small group was sent to carry out the wounded, all of whom had relatively minor wounds in the limbs, and bring back supplies. The men returned a short while later with bad news. The area was swarming with enemy troops and the detail was unable to get the wounded through, or obtain necessary supplies and ammo. What was worse, the leg wound casualties had died on the way down, not from the severity of their wounds, but from the effects of shock and the extreme cold. Here in Korea, even minor flesh wounds were often lethal, made so by the killer cold.

The unit braced for the worst. Contemplating the worsening situation, and unable to get needed supplies, Baker Company waited in uneasiness. Finally, the radio burst to life with welcome news, "Baker Six, Baker Six, this is Red Six. Get your fannies back here as quickly as possible!"

The unit carefully made their way through the frozen expanse of enemy territory and back to the Chipyong-ni perimeter. It was 12 February 1951, the eve of a great battle that could determine the fate of an entire war.

CHAPTER XIII
UNDER SIEGE

When Baker Company finally made it back safely to the friendly perimeter, they were returned to Regimental reserve force duty. While they had been out on Hill 506, things had been rapidly heating up for units of the X Corps to whom the 2nd Division was now attached. As regimental reserve force, Baker Company combat leaders were ordered to recon the defensive positions along the entire Chipyong-ni perimeter, to familiarize themselves with the places they may be called to defend in a moment's notice.

About 20 miles to the northeast, nearly 14 miles north of Wonju, the forward ROK troops who were staged to launch an attack, were hit with a massive enemy assault. The 9th RCT at Sogu was made ready to withdraw 13 miles to Yoju. Elements of the 38th RCT deployed in support of the pending ROK assault fell under heavy attack by 0300 and were withdrawing under massive fire all along their route. Arial recon had found the enemies main assault force streaming down the main road from Hongchon and splitting off in two directions: one strait south toward Wonju, and the other breaking west toward Chipyong-ni.

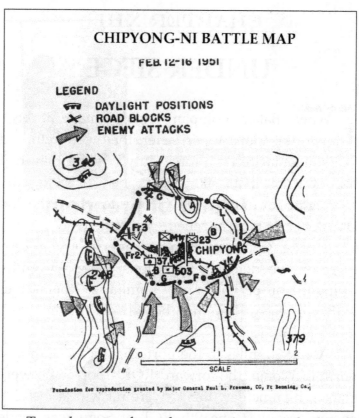

Two hours after the massive attack began against the forward ROK units; four CCF Divisions had decimated the South Korean forces, inflicting over 8,000 casualties. The allied teams deployed to support the ROK units were cut off from them and now taking major assaults themselves. The 38th was on the run, pulling back amid a deluge of mortar and small arms fire. Trucks were being destroyed leaving many units to retreat on foot. The 1st and 3rd Battalions of the 38th RCT joined forces at the bridge at Haktam-ni, while the enemy worked to set up roadblocks to their south to prevent their escape.

The 3rd Battalion held as rear guard as the 1st began its escape under a heavy curtain of allied air and artillery support. The 1st couldn't break through on its own and the 3rd soon fell back to join them. The two battered Battalions slowly made their way while under murderous enemy fire from the hills along the roadsides. A short distance south, Brigadier General Stewart, the assistant 2nd Division commander arrived in Wonju and took command to defend the city. A defensive perimeter was set up and artillery was staged to hammer every approach. By midnight, what remained of the 1st and 3rd Battalions of the 38th RCT crawled into Wonju. They had suffered 1,400 casualties this day.

Weaknesses on the Chipyong-ni Perimeter?

Miles to the west, the 23rd Regimental Combat Team were bracing for what would soon come. While soldiers continued to prep for battle, the combat leaders of Baker Company had completed their recon of the perimeter. With respectful caution the Baker Company Commander, Capt. Sherman Pratt, made his report to Regimental staff, denoting many substandard fighting positions found along the 2nd Battalion line comprising the southern ridge of the perimeter ring. Pratt's concerns were that if heavily hit, the fighting positions were too shallow and improperly placed for a solid defense, and if his men were called to occupy those same positions, they too would be in jeopardy. The 2nd Battalion Commander was furious that a junior officer would question his leadership. The danger, because it was pointed out by a junior officer, was apparently disregarded, and later came back to haunt.

A Perilous Predicament

The forced withdrawals of the 9th and 38th RCT's too far south of where the 23rd RCT was now entrenched placed the 23rd truly out on a limb. They were now isolated at Chipyong-ni, in a circular defense in a peninsula like bulge in the allied defensive line. Arial recon and intelligence reports were showing that the enemy was rapidly pouring into the area, and the Regiment was fast becoming surrounded by vastly superior numbers.

Col. Freeman was confident of his troop's capabilities, and therefore never afraid to make a stand, but a good commander always looked at the odds for success before making any decision. To fall under siege against a vastly larger enemy force, that would also have them surrounded a great distance from any reinforcements, was going against his better judgment. He petitioned Corps commanders for permission to make an immediate withdrawal, before withdrawal was impossible.

The answer was "no". Word was that General Matthew Ridgeway was frustrated with the allied forces being forced to withdraw every time they faced a massive concentration of enemy forces. The question was there: could allied forces, properly prepared, stand and prevail against the numerically superior CCF forces? Other higher commanders agreed that it was time to put the Chinese to the test. This time, there would be no withdrawal. It is said Col. Freeman agreed, though he thought a little better odds and better terrain to work with should be the scene of such a venture. But nonetheless, the 23rd would valiantly make their stand; come what may - even their own annihilation.

The Test Begins

13 February. The day's patrols had reported greatly increased enemy activity in the area close to the perimeter, particularly in the North, East, and West sides. The 2nd Recon unit found 1,000 enemy troops moving from the southeast toward the main road leading to Chipyong-ni.

As the skies over Chipyong-ni dimmed and night began to close in, CPL Chet Thiessen watched and listened as the glow of red and green enemy flares began to light the sky, and all around the 23rd RCT perimeter the sound of bugles and whistles could be heard, amidst the din of banging and clanking of metal on metal. The enemy was there, and they wanted them to know it. The 23rd Regiment was surrounded, and any help was a long way off. Every soldier anxiously waited and watched in the cold dusk, checking to be sure their rifles worked freely, reaching to their ammo belts again and again to reassure themselves that the bullets they put their earlier were still close at hand; reluctantly drawing the last drag on their cigarettes, wondering if it would be their last, knowing that what they did in the hours ahead would determine their fate - perhaps the fate of an entire war - and it all rested on their shoulders.

At 2200 hours, out of the northeast, north, and southeast small arms and mortar fire began to rain on the perimeter. A short time later, a barrage of enemy artillery and mortar fire fell on the 1st Battalion positions on the northern section of the circle. Suddenly the barrage ceased and the long awaited attack by the enemy troops crashed against the defenders of the 1st Battalion.

The night came alive as the fireworks of thousands of tracer rounds lit the air, raking the defensive lines. The 1st Battalion command post burned as the fighting spread all around the perimeter, until all units were engaged. The fortifications so carefully prepared by most units on the perimeter protected friendly fighters while they inflicted massive casualties on the fanatically attacking human waves of the Chinese hordes.

While the defenders fought the enemy onslaught, an incessant and heavy rain of enemy mortar and artillery fell everywhere inside the perimeter. The hellish deluge prevented the evacuation of wounded as even the aid station was under heavy fire. The Regimental command post was hit by several rounds. Members of the Regimental staff were killed, and the Regimental commander, Colonel Paul Freeman, was wounded by shrapnel.

When midnight came, the fighting let up slightly, but a new enemy attack came at 0100. The screaming hordes hit and were again repulsed by the defenders. The soldiers on the perimeter listened in the night to the sounds of shovels striking the dirt. The enemy was digging in. The siege of Chipyong-ni was on, and the enemy was planning to stay.

At 0215, the brunt of the attack moved to the 3rd Battalion sector. "K" Company absorbed the worst of the thrust, but held strong, holding off wave after wave of raging masses. Next the enemy charged the southern section and that of the French forces, trying in vain to pierce the allied perimeter defenses. Massive waves of enemy from the northwest sector plowed into the French and "C" Company lines, driving them back slightly, but immediate counterattacks shoved the enemy back and regained any lost ground.

The entire circle around Chipyong-ni glowed as if afire with unceasing blasts from both friendly and unfriendly weapons. The 23rd forces literally poured round after round of artillery and mortar fire onto the raging enemy masses charging the iron ring of defenders. Blood flowed in torrents as the enemy dead piled up all around the perimeter. By 0530, after a night of incessant combat, the weight of the attack eased slightly except for on the east and west sides where the French and K Company continued to fight savagely.

As morning dawned on the 14th, another major enemy thrust rammed against the eastern circle, with K and I Companies of the 3rd Battalion giving no ground. The days spent hardening the positions of the defensive perimeter had paid off. For all of the vicious combat, for now the 23rd's casualty count was low. But the siege was far from over. Five Chinese Divisions now surrounded the 23rd Regiment. Finally, under fear of air strikes permitted by the now growing daylight and murderous mortar and artillery fire already being sent their way, the enemy pulled back temporarily, leaving only harassing mortar fire in their wake.

The "Wonju Shoot"

No story of Chipyong-ni would be complete without detailing what happened at the same time at Wonju, to the east, on 14 February where other elements of the 2nd Division were also engaged in bitter fighting. When morning dawned, aerial observers found two enemy Divisions moving along the Som River in formations meant to surround the defenders at Wonju. The 2nd Division called every cannon to bear they possessed or could otherwise obtain in supportive fire.

Hellfire rained from the sky upon the enemy troops in a massive barrage the likes of which had never before been seen to fall upon any enemy army in history. As the explosion of thousands of shells thundered, and their steel shrapnel ripped and shredded the mass of Chinese soldiers, they still marched forward as if oblivious of the slaughter all around them. Pilots observing the carnage overhead reported that the river itself had turned red with the blood that poured from the dead of the enemy hordes.

The massacre continued for hours as allied artillerymen struggled in exhaustion to feed their glowing red barrels that shouted death to the enemy. The enemy masses began to thin out, and soon confusion and despair replaced their courage. Finally, useless, staggering bands of bewildered enemy troops began to run away, trying in vain to escape their fate as the air assault picked up where the artillery left off as the retreating enemy escaped the range of the cannons. Massed artillery had proven its worth against the raging Chinese hordes.

What had been deemed the "Wonju Shoot" had cost the enemy 5,000 lives in a matter of hours.

But the enemy was far from done. Turned back at Wonju, they shifted both their troops and the focus of all of their attention on the near frozen and dog tired, 23rd Regiment besieged at Chipyong-ni.

Readying for another Long Night

The defenders at Chipyong-ni were hard at work to repair the damage wrought by the attacks of the previous night. Wounded were cared for, and the most critical were med-evac'd by helicopter while the opportunity existed before nightfall. Weary soldiers cleared the frozen enemy dead bodies and battle debris from their fighting positions. Entrenching tools chopped at the frozen dirt that had poured into many a foxhole sent in the backlash of brutal explosions. Either too tired to speak or lost in thought, the combat hardened men worked silently, steadily, efficiently, with the knowledge that this battle was far from over, and soon the enemy would come again.

And come they did, attacking at different times throughout the day around the perimeter defenses, keeping up the pressure to continually wear down our already exhausted troops while testing for weaknesses in the, as yet, iron circle of the 23rd that they could exploit later.

Aviators Give All in Desperate Resupply Effort

With the entire 23rd Regimental Combat Team under siege, and the long night of vicious combat, supplies of ammo were more than critically low. The only option available for resupply was by massive air drops that consisted of 24 sorties flown by teams of C-119 Flying Boxcars on the afternoon of February 14th. The big planes were forced to come in low, open their tail doors, and pull up quickly to allow the precious cargo to drop by parachute into the small ring of defenders.

"I always loved airplanes, and watched with fascination as the supply planes flew in. The problem was that they had to come in so low to drop the supplies, on us, and not give them to the enemy, and the planes were so big that they were easy targets. There were overwhelming amounts of enemy soldiers' hitting us all around - we were terribly outnumbered, and the only way to keep them back was with mortar and artillery support. It would have been impossible to stop firing. There were constant mortar barrages by the enemy at different places around the perimeter, and the planes were so low that when they came in over the hills the enemy could easily hit them even with their small arms fire.

If I remember right, I counted 11 of the big planes shot down that day. From what I could see they were flying right in to the mortar and artillery crossfire in the air from both sides. After the first couple planes were shot down I'm sure the rest of the pilots and crews knew they had little chance of getting out alive, but they came in anyway, literally giving their lives to get the desperately needed ammo and supplies to us. I don't know if that's ever been written anywhere."

In spite of the heroic resupply effort, the ammo stocks were still dangerously low, especially 8-round clips for the M-1 rifles.[8] Every bullet was already issued out and none remained in reserve.

A Change of Command under Fire

As helicopters continually dodged bullets ferrying the wounded out, another brought a different cargo. LTC John Chiles, the Corps G-3, had arrived to relieve 23rd Regiment Commander COL

---

[8] One after action report notes that the wrong ammo had been dropped. According to the recollection of Chet Thiessen, pistol ammunition had been inadvertently dropped in place of rifle ammo.

Paul Freeman who had been seriously wounded during the previous night's devastating mortar barrage on the Regimental command post.

Freeman adamantly refused to leave his men and, ignoring Chiles, continued to command his troops. The helicopter sent to carry Freeman out, coming under heavy fire, couldn't wait any longer and left without him. Freeman continued to refuse to abandon his troops in the middle of the battle. Finally another helicopter arrived, and apparently with it, direct orders, insisting COL Freeman stand down and evacuate to the aid station for medical treatment.

Chet Thiessen remembers, "I was one of the stretcher bearers who carried my Colonel to the helicopter. I read somewhere that he was wounded in the knee by shrapnel. That's not where I remember the bandages; I could swear they were on his backside. I suppose it's more dignified though for an officer to get wounded in the 'knee' instead. Nonetheless we were sad to see him go."

Amidst the constant barrages from enemy mortar, artillery, and self-propelled guns, the new 23rc RCT commander was ominously greeted by late afternoon reports of increasing enemy activity all around the perimeter.

CHAPTER XIV
A TIME TO STAND OR DIE

At 2030 hours on February 14th, the Communist Chinese bloodlust resurged; out of the frozen darkness unleashing a heavy mortar barrage on the 3rd Battalion holding the east side of the perimeter, and opening fire on the 1st Battalion sector from the north. "C" Company on the northern rim reported they could hear sounds of the enemy digging in out in the darkness. Shortly after, a major assault of enemy forces slammed the 2nd Battalion sector while the Regimental Command was pounded by massive mortar, artillery, and small arms fire that eventually hindered the friendly mortar positions ability to fire in support of the line units.

To the sound of enemy bugles, the fighting rose quickly in crescendo about the beleaguered enclave of defenders. Seemingly in response to the same potential defensive weaknesses identified along the 2nd Battalion line the day before by Baker Company commander Captain Pratt, the 2nd and 3rd Battalion section came under massive enemy assault with close combat action occurring all along the line as the Communist forces sought to drive a wedge into the perimeter to divide the defending forces and enable the enemy to attack them from front and back at the same time. To confuse and complicate the situation, Chinese 120mm mortar shells rained down with malice on the Regimental command.

Finally, though friendly artillery continued to pursue them, the unsuccessful Communist attack subsided briefly as the Chinese pulled back and regrouped for another try at the now exhausted 23rd infantry.

Battering Rams at the Gates

By 0130 two massive assaults by the Chinese hordes had been driven back by 3rd Battalions "K" company on the southeast sector, as other assaults continued their attempts to drive into the southern perimeter. Finally, about 0230, "I" Company positions on the east side were penetrated by overwhelming waves of Chinese troops, and driven back. "L" Company joined with "I" Company soldiers in an immediate counter attack brutally shoving the Chinese back, in up close and personal hand-to-hand combat, regaining the lost ground by literally using their bayonets to dig the enemy out of their foxholes.

The intrepid defenders held their ground. However, though driven on with stubbornness and will; still subject to the limitations of human biology, the men were wearing down. Completely surrounded, outnumbered five to one, in the cold blackness of a frozen winter night, short of every kind of ammunition, and tired to the bone; could the soldiers of the 23rd continue to hold?

The ammunition situation that was already dangerous had now become critical. Could the 23rd's ammo last until daylight? A radio cry for help went out to Japan Logistical Command, whose air crews worked all through the night loading planes with ammo for an emergency air-drop at daybreak, while the battle for Chipyong-ni raged on through the night.

Enemy Breach

Shortly after 0300, disaster struck. The defenses began to crumble along the 2nd Battalion perimeter on the southern sector. "G" Company and a part of "E" Company were overwhelmed by the Communist hordes. The small handful of men that remained of "G" Company were driven from their positions and forced to pull back.

Every soldier and commander understood what the perimeter breach meant. If they didn't, they soon had a lesson as the Chinese now had a clear visibility and a line of fire from the high ground into the defensive perimeter. At any moment the Communist commanders could realize their advantage and send virtual rivers of soldiers down into the enclosure and divide and attack the 23rd's positions from the rear. If that happened, the battle would likely be over, along with the lives of the 23rd infantry, and maybe the entire war.

Quickly assessing the situation, Regimental Commander John Chiles immediately ordered a counter-attack, sending the 1st Ranger Company from Regimental reserve to join with the small handful of able bodied men remaining of "G" Company, and a platoon freed up from "F" Company fighting on the G Company flank to repulse the enemy from the precious high ground and retake the G Company positions. At the same time, "A" and "C" Companies were viciously beating back human waves of Chinese troops on the northern rim.

CPL Chet Thiessen waited anxiously with the rest of Baker Company for the inevitable orders to move out to reinforce the line anywhere and at any time. The Ranger Company's commitment to the counter attack now left only Baker Company in reserve. Chet had a good idea of what to expect as he had led his squad to many places around the perimeter since the battle started to fill critical gaps in the line with .30 caliber machine gun fire. Baker Company had already suffered many casualties from the constant enemy mortar barrages. While they impatiently waited to join the fray once more, bayonets were sharpened, gear was checked over and over, ammo and grenades secured. The blackness of the frozen Korean winter night was all afire with tracer bullets, exploding shells, and fire belching cannons. These men were more than ready to get on the line and start sending some lead of their own downrange.

In the meantime the Communist forces weren't standing around waiting for the 2nd Battalion counter-attack to happen. From their newly established advantage on the high ground, they pounded the command posts with mortar fire and hosed the fire support teams down with automatic weapon fire. To make matters worse, the 23rd Infantry was almost out of ammo. Only a few mortar rounds remained. The entire Regiment was ordered to only shoot at what they knew they could hit.

Units of the 503rd Field Artillery within range of the southern perimeter breach suddenly came under heavy small arms fire and had to abandon their artillery pieces, effectively preventing fire support for the counter attacking force. The perimeter breach was critical. The defenses were in extreme jeopardy. They had to move before the Chinese figured that out. Before it was too late.

Relief Forces on the Way

Approximately seven miles south of Chipyong-ni, COL Marcel Crombez, commander of the 5th Calvary Regiment was called to organize a task force of tanks and infantry to break through the enemy lines to disrupt the siege and help relieve the beleaguered 23rd Infantry.

Crombez' tanks, laden with infantry troops battled up the main road through an enemy gauntlet reminiscent of Kunu-ri two months before. A veritable slaughter of the exposed infantry passengers commenced as they fought desperately and valiantly forward through the crossfire of enemy troops from both sides of the road. Dead American soldiers fell from the blood drenched tanks as the hot lead of enemy weapons pinged and pounded against the steadily forward rolling iron war machines. Tank cannons roared into the night as they fired point blank into the Communist forces assailing them. Blood flowed freely on both sides.

If the relief force didn't make it through to the besieged troops by nightfall, they would be surrounded and stranded in the open amidst the thousands of Chinese forces currently encircling Chipyong-ni. Failure could have lethal consequences for both the 5th Calvary and the besieged 23rd.

The Second Counter-attack Fails

At 0615 the counter attack force composed of Rangers and elements of "F" and "G" Companies charged forward against the Communist forces to retake the critical high ground the enemy had recently wrested from them. The Chinese though were not going to let go of their advantage that easily. Brutal and bloody hand to hand combat ensued until the counter attacking force finally had to pull back to Chipyong-ni with nearly 100% casualties. The enemy held their ground and continued their onslaught of fire upon the 23rd's positions within the perimeter.

At the same time, Colonel Crombez and his cavalry armor and infantry continued to pound their way to Chipyong-ni. They were still taking heavy fire and moving slowly in the process. If the soldiers at Chipyong-ni could not retake the critical high ground they had lost on the southern rim, the 5th Cav. may be sitting ducks with the vast enemy forces holding the commanding terrain on both sides of the narrow pass his tanks needed to pass through. It may even be found impossible to actually get through to the friendly forces, especially if the armored column couldn't make it by dark. They continued their slow push forward against the tide of massive resistance. The clock was ticking.

Baker Company Comes to the Rescue

Amidst the deafening background noise of exploding incoming enemy mortar and artillery rounds and the defensive gunfire the Baker Company commander's radio suddenly crackled to life. Baker Company was to move out immediately to the 2nd Battalion area to mount the next counter attack to retake the lost high-ground. Without it, there was little hope in getting the reinforcing Calvary units through, blasting their way north to come to the aid of the beleaguered defenders at Chipyong-ni.

Two entire company strength units had been nearly been wiped out in the previous attempts to drive the tenacious and numerous Communist forces from the heights they were exploiting to rain hell on the interior of the Chipyong-ni perimeter. The only ones left to do it was Sherman Pratt's Baker Company, and CPL Chet Thiessen, Bernie Cartee, and Roy Anderson were among those intrepid soldiers that rushed across the enclave that morning to make a last, desperate attempt to literally pry the Chinese from their positions and secure the perimeter defenses before the enemy made another massive human wave thrust into the defensive ring and presented our troops with impossible odds of survival.

Uncomfortable Alliance

As Baker Company made its way to the 2nd Battalion area on the southern rim of the battered perimeter they passed through the 503rd Field Artillery positions to find the Artillerymen under cover behind their massive guns unable to lend fire support because they were now coming under heavy enemy fire from the now compromised high ground.

In spite of the battle raging all around, as the Baker Company commander strode into the 2nd Battalion command bunker, there was clearly uneasiness in the air. Only two days before, Captain Pratt had reported the findings of his recon of the 23rd Infantry defensive positions to regimental commanders, specifically noting that many of the 2nd Battalion defensive positions on the southern rim may not be adequate and presented a potential weakness in the Chipyong-ni defenses. Now that same junior officer had been sent to retake those same positions that had been breached by the Chinese, leaving the fate of the 23rd infantry hanging in the wind.

In spite of the personal tensions that existed, there was no time to waste in mounting the counter attack to retake the lost ground. At any moment the Communist forces could realize their advantage and send wave after wave of enemy troops surging through the breach and into the weakened enclosure. The counter attack had to succeed.

CHAPTER XV

A MEDAL OF HONOR

After the tenuous briefing at the 2nd Battalion Command Post, Captain Pratt relayed the desperation of the situation to his combat leaders while they all hugged the ground as a hail of enemy machine gun fire tore at the ground around them. Baker Company was the last hope for a successful counter attack. Without it the relief force may never get through, and the danger of being overrun was so extreme at this point as to be beyond description. Baker rallied and moved out under heavy fire in a deliberate and meticulous drive forward. CPL Chet Thiessen, along with Anderson and Cartee were sent out on the flank where G Company had been driven back twice.

As Baker Company slowly drove forward while taking heavy casualties, Chet Thiessen and his team came upon a harrowing sight. They found the remnants of the defenders on the G Company line battle worn and weary. There was enemy gunfire shouting loudly, but few of the friendly forces were firing back. Instead they all were focusing their attention on something happening in the distance.

About a hundred yards out in front of them in the frozen white of an open rice paddy lay a dead American D Company machine gunner slumped over his .30 caliber machine gun, who had apparently been killed when the perimeter had been overrun by the Chinese earlier. The three young soldiers watched in awe as they saw what was transpiring. The enemy had stopped firing at the exhausted and beaten soldiers on the line, and were concentrating their fire, in some intentional and macabre desecration, on the dead machine gunners body out in the open, ripping it to shreds. The Communist troops were close enough that their taunts and laughter could be heard in the frigid air.

As the Baker Company machine gun team quickly slid over the frozen earth and down into the nearest fighting position, they all had been in combat long enough to realize the significance of what was happening. After three days of nearly nonstop combat, and being nearly wiped out in the previous hours two failed counter attacks, the devastatingly exhausted and battered remnants of the troops on the line were giving in to the cold and combat fatigue. These valiant soldiers, in the wake of combat fatigue on the frozen battlefield, were losing their will to fight. The demoralizing scene before them as the enemy sought to destroy the hallowed remains of a fallen fellow soldier, was the last straw. The last of the perimeter defenses were collapsing. If the enemy rushed the positions now, the entire section of the line would inevitably fall, men would die, and hardly a shot would be fired to prevent it.

When Heroes Rise Up

The imminent danger was not lost on the combat leaders present. Upon seeing the new B Company machine gun team arrive, two officers quickly made their way to them.

"Corporal," the commander appealed anxiously to Chet Thiessen through visible exhaustion, "somebody has to do something! If you can get to that dead gunner out there and get his body to cover, we'll do whatever it takes to see that you get the Medal of Honor!"

As the two officers waited in anticipation of his answer, the young 18 year old Corporal quickly contemplated the situation. He looked at the gaunt and exhausted faces of his fellow soldiers, wounded, and battered inside and out almost beyond human endurance, then to the dead body in the distance of his brother machine gunner being torn to shreds by the bloodlust of the Chinese Communists who were ravaging from their vantage point the interior of the perimeter defenses, then to his buddies Cartee and Anderson, and back to the waiting stares of the two officers.

Realizing the danger to the men of his regiment, and the near suicidal task that he had been asked to volunteer for, for a brief moment his thoughts went to his mother and other family waiting for him back in Grand Rapids, when all the defiance and tenacity that had preserved him throughout his young life came together all at this moment. Rage and hatred rose up inside him for the enemy that had tortured him only weeks before while a Prisoner of War, who were desecrating his fellow machine gunners body, and threatened his friends who daily fought at his side. Again, he dared the enemy to beat him.

"I'll go." He said, already handing his .30 caliber machine gun to Cartee and quickly shedding his combat gear to make himself a much smaller target. Both Cartee and Anderson stood by in knowing silence, realizing that they may never see their friend again respecting the magnitude of what they understood he was about to do. "I'll need that Thompson." He said motioning to the officers Thompson machine gun he carried.

Without hesitation, Thompson in hand, .45 at his side, and his prized blue handled Turkish combat knife, a gift to him from a soldier in a Turkish unit, slid into his combat boot, 18 year old Chet Thiessen lunged up and over the side of the foxhole and into the open.

Sliding over the spent brass shell casings, grenade pins and other war debris, past the now motionless and silent dead bodies of several fellow soldiers that had fallen earlier that day, he was now totally exposed and hugging the ground in a death defying low crawl across the wide frozen rice paddy making his way the long football field distance to rescue the remains of a fellow soldier, and hopefully save the lives of what may be hundreds more in the process.

Baker Company gets Pinned Down

Elsewhere the rest of Baker Company drove forward toward the targeted high ground in their counter offensive. The amount of their dead and wounded mounted, and soon their reserve platoon was called forward to make up the difference. The enemy held on tenaciously.

When the Baker Company troops had pushed to their side of the crest of the hill, they found themselves in an unusual stalemate. They were pinned down on their side of the hill just below the hilltop, and the enemy was also pinned down on their side of the hilltop. Neither could see each other, but both were close enough to trade handgrenades, and this is how the offensive commenced. Every time Baker tried to charge over the hill, they were easily cut down.

In this situation, artillery support was out of the question. Both the American and Chinese troops were so close to each other, the risk of friendly fire falling on our own men was too great. Baker commander Captain Pratt called for tank support hoping the mobility of the tanks could place them in a position to strike at the other side of the slope where the enemy was entrenched in the fighting positions formerly occupied by the 2nd Battalion soldiers only hours before. The 23rd Regiment tank units kicked up clouds of dust in the distance and spun their way onto the road heading in Baker Company's direction. Suddenly, a massive explosion thundered beneath the lead tank. Any tank support from their tank support units was out of the question now too, as the Chinese had found a way to mine the road with anti-tank mines during the night.

Captain Pratt finally called for an air strike. The hope was that a Napalm drop on the far slope of the hill would cause enough damage to the enemy troops while the crest of the hill shielded the friendly forces, to allow what was left of Baker Company to charge over the top and drive the remnant enemy from their positions, securing once again the desperately needed objective. It was getting late, and time was running out for the 23rd defenders and the 5th Cavalry relief force pounding their way in from the south.

The American Spirit

Chet Thiessen hugged the ground tightly as he slid as quickly as possible across the frozen waste. The ice and snow burned the side of his face and his knees and elbows, but he kept moving.

When the soldiers nearby noticed what was happening, they all stirred quickly to watch Chet Thiessen's advance across the ice. As American's tend to do for their team, some began to cheer him on, willing him to victory.

As soon as the enemy heard the commotion, they hesitated in their demoralizing onslaught on the remains of the dead D Company gunner. Then they did what enemies do when challenged. They began to turn all their fire on a different target; now the young Corporal crawling toward them in the open.

The ice and snow suddenly erupted all around him as thousands of rounds of enemy automatic weapon fire reached out to kill him in his tracks. Chet flinched and blinked as the stinging shards of ice tore at his face, sent flying from the rain of lead falling all about him. But instead of deterring him in his quest, it only made him mad.

As images flashed through his mind of his weeks of torture and beatings while a Chinese prisoner, his defiance rose up en masse.

"You think you can kill me?" He screamed as he continually moved closer to the enemy, "You can't kill me! I won't let you kill me you bastards!" Despite the bullets coming close enough to pull at his clothing, he moved faster and with more determination.

Friendly forces nearby were beginning to rise up with renewed vigor, seeming to forget the despair they exhibited only minutes before. The American spirit bred into them had only been dampened for a time by human weakness and now began to resurge, as they witnessed the indomitable spirit and intrepid actions of Chet Thiessen. The pain of their wounds and the debilitation of fatigue and cold were waning. They cheered on their brother, who was now engulfed by a bloodthirsty hellstorm before them, in defiance of their hated enemy.

With his body pressed so close to the ground he nearly became part of it he skidded along, finally coming in contact with something solid with his outstretched hand. He carefully turned his gaze to see the boot of the dead machine gunner right in front of him.

A sense of relief came over him in spite of the murderous tumult all around that he had finally reached his goal and would hopefully be skidding back to the safety of friendly lines any minute. Slipping the strap of the Thompson machine gun over his arm, he reached out with both hands and tried to pull the dead body, slumped over the now destroyed .30 caliber back to him. But there was a problem. The bloody remains had frozen to the machine gun and the ice around it. This body wasn't coming loose either, not without help.

"Oh this is great, now what?" Chet thought to himself as a shot of panicked adrenaline raced through his body. He had crawled all this way under fire with the hope of saving the body of his brother machine gunner from desecration, and the morale and lives of his fellow soldiers he could still faintly hear cheering him over the massive battle noise that shook the air all about him. Now he found himself pinned to the icy ground by an onslaught of enemy lead that had his name written all over it, with the body frozen solidly in place, well above him, fully in the line of fire. If he failed now, what would happen to the battered defenders hundreds of feet behind who found in him and what he was doing, sudden and renewed spirit? If he failed now, what would happen to the hundreds of men of the 23rd Regiment if the Chinese broke into the perimeter through a shattered and broken defensive line?

With his face pressed against the ice beneath him, he closed his eyes tightly and thought, blocking out everything around him. "What do I do?" he asked himself, no doubt sending up that same question at the same time in a desperate prayer for guidance. In a split second, his life, his family back home, and the present situation flashed before his mind's eye. Then in a moment of the greatest resolve, everything went quiet, and all thinking stopped. If he was going to die today, he was going to die fighting . . .

The Decisive Moment

In spite of the hail of led thundering all around him, with complete disregard for his own life, Chet Thiessen suddenly raised himself up fully exposing himself to the enemy onslaught of hot lead in order to quickly pry the frozen remains from the machine gun. After freeing it from the big gun, a few quick tugs and the body came free from the ice around it. After what seemed like hours literally sitting in the bull's-eye of hundreds of enemy gun barrels pointed directly at him, he began his long, desperate low crawl back to the friendly line with the body of his brother machine gunner in tow.

As friendly troops watched in awe at the events transpiring before them, Chet moved as fast as possible with his fallen buddy back to the safety of cover and friendly forces. Taking a quick look back over his shoulder, he saw to his dismay that his prized blue handled combat knife given to him in friendship by a Turkish soldier had slipped from its home in his boot and lay in the distance on the ice. That knife had saved his life many times, but there was no going back to get it now. Onward he pushed.

Near friendly positions he came across some small rocks protruding through the ice. He crawled over to them with the body and carefully, without lifting his own body pinned down under fire on the open ice, slid the body of his brother soldier up and behind the stones where it would be safe from any further harm.

"There you go bud, rest in peace, you'll be safe here now," the young Corporal said silently, then skidded as fast as possible back and over the edge of the fighting position where Cartee and Anderson were anxiously waiting for him.

After a few seconds of back slaps of welcome greeting by soldiers all around, Bernard Cartee, grabbing Chet by the shoulder, exclaimed, "Chet, you sure as heck better get the Medal of Honor for what you just did! I can't believe you're not laying out there in pieces!"

Though he was ever so grateful to be back behind friendly lines, Chet's focus wasn't on the welcoming committee. His heart was racing from the adrenalin rush of what he had just experienced. The sound of his heart beating was all he could hear at the moment through a strange ringing in his ears. This wasn't done yet. Quickly grabbing his .30 caliber machine gun from Roy Anderson, he cried out, "Let's move!"

While a startled Cartee and Anderson watched in disbelief, the battle ravaged young Corporal racked the bolt back on his weapon and charged screaming out of the fox hole firing at the enemy. With Cartee and Anderson on his heels, and the newly rallied defenders on his section of the line, Chet Thiessen led a savage and desperate counter attack against the Chinese troops who only moments before had sought to destroy him. Firing the air cooled .30 from the hip he led the charge across the open expanse of ice, taking a heavy toll on the enemy. Finally this last desperate counter attack by the newly inspired haggard remnants of the American defenders successfully drove the Chinese from their positions in a bloody and brutal close combat.

Baker Over the Top

While Chet Thiessen and his team fought madly for their new positions on the defensive line, elsewhere, the rest of Baker Company was pinned down and inching their way up to the hilltop before them. The napalm strike called for earlier finally hit the enemy positions on the far side of the hill. It landed somewhat far down the slope, but its fiery wrath spread far and wide distracting the enemy for the critical moments it took the screaming remnants of Baker Company to charge over the crest of the hill with guns ablaze sending a murderous curtain of lead that drove the rattled and smoldering enemy troops from the 2nd Battalion fighting positions and forced them into a stumbling and desperate running retreat down the hill in disarray.

At 1630 hours Baker Company dove into the now re-secured fighting positions and quickly cleared the charred and bloody remains of enemy dead from the bunkers to make room to stand their defensive against any immediate enemy counterattack, the 5th Cavalry relief force could now be seen in the distance pounding their way in to aid the besieged 23rd Infantry. The surging 5th Cavalry armor now trained their cannon on the retreating enemy, raining down fire and steel on the confused enemy who began an all-out retreat. Not to be outdone, the big guns of the 23rd Infantry turned about to join in the fray and sent their own manner of hellfire in a devastating artillery barrage onto the backs of the exposed and frantically fleeing Communist forces.

Cease Fire

By 1700, with nearly every bullet and artillery shell completely used up, the Regimental Commander called for a cease fire. A few minutes later, the 5th Cavalry armored relief force jubilantly rolled into the perimeter.

At 2000 hours, Baker Company Commander Sherman Pratt's radio crackled softly in the frigid night air with a whisper of welcome news: the 2nd Battalion troops would take over, and Baker was to pull back to positions closer to town. With nearly half the unit wiped out, the exhausted and wounded remnants of Baker Company slowly made their way back through the night.

The Turning Point

In almost three days of non-stop combat, the men of the 23rd Regimental Combat Team had stood toe-to-toe with an overwhelming force of as many as five Chinese Communist Divisions. United Nations forces had proved they could stand in the face of everything the enemy could throw at them, and prevail. Though the outcome of the battle had hung in uncertainty for critical moments, the Communist forces had been severely routed, and had, at least for the next few days, literally disappeared from the battlefield to lick their wounds. A new chapter in the war had begun.

PRESIDENTIAL DISTINGUISHED UNIT CITATION

23rd Regimental Combat Team

In the name of the President of the United States as public evidence of deserved honor and distinction of the 23rd Regimental Combat Team, 2nd Infantry Division, comprised of the following units:

  23rd Infantry Regiment
  37th Field Artillery Battalion
  "B" Battery, 82nd AAA Battalion
  "B" Battery, 503rd Field Artillery Battalion
  "B" Company, 2nd Engineer Battalion
  2d Clearing Pltn, Clearing Co., 2d Medical Battalion
  1st Infantry Ranger Company

Is cited for extraordinary heroism in combat near Chipyong-ni, Korea, during the period 13 through 15 February 1951. These units, comprising a regimental combat team, were disposed in a defensive perimeter around Chipyong-ni with the hazardous mission of holding this important communications center and denying the enemy its extensive road net. On 13 February, hordes of Chinese Communist troops launched many determined attacks from every quarter, strongly supported by heavy mortar and artillery fire. Prearranged fire with artillery, tanks and mortars hurled back these fanatical assaults until the morning of 14 February when the enemy separated the 23rd Regimental Combat Team from supporting units to the south, entirely surrounded it, and made resupply possible only by air drop. Because of the encircling force, estimated to be four Chinese communist divisions, the Chipyong-ni perimeter rapidly developed into a "stand-or-die" defense. Fierce hand-to-hand combat engaged the two forces in the evening of the second day of the siege and only one company remained in reserve. With ammunition stocks running low, this one remaining unit was committed on 15 February and waves of attacking Chinese communists again were stemmed. Shortly after noon on 15 February, radio contact was established with a relief force and friendly tanks broke through the enemy encirclement and forced his withdrawal. The dogged determination, gallantry and indomitable spirit displayed by the 23rd Regimental Combat Team when completely surrounded and cut off, the destruction of attacking Chinese communist hordes which enabled the United Nations Forces to maintain their front, resume the offensive, and the steadfast and stubborn refusal to allow a fanatical and numerically superior force to dislodge them are in keeping with the finest traditions of the United States Army and reflect great credit on all members of the units who participated in this historical combat action.

CHAPTER XVI

A PURPLE HEART

After the tenacious and decisive battle at Chipyong-ni, there were no vacations taken. New strategies and operations were put in place now that allied forces had found that the Chinese Communists were not all they were cracked up to be. "Operation Killer" for the 2nd Division jumped off on 22 February 1951. The zone of responsibility assigned to the 2nd Division contained tremendous terrain challenges resulting in miserable advances from one steep ridgeline to another.

177

New problems arose. The advancing units in the steep, remote and tenuous terrain were having extremely difficult re-supply operations to add to their physical challenges. These problems made it nearly impossible to complete their objectives. A program using native Koreans as supply train bearers to carry desperately needed supplies to the advancing troops was established, while air drops laid out rations and ammunition to troops in the remotest locations. In spite of all the difficulties, the forward advance continued on.

The first of March found the Division driving forward toward a goal marked the "Arizona Line", passing east to west through Hyonch'on-ni, that was the first in a series of planned phases of advance. Up and over one steep and rugged hill after another the men of the 23rd Infantry trudged one exhausting, freezing step at a time.

The 7th of March found Chet Thiessen with his unit stepping off from the Arizona Line in the latest "Operation Ripper" that was geared and planned to move the Allied forces to the 38th parallel. The units would fight tenaciously to drive the Reds from every ridgeline only to find them dug in on the next one behind it. Though the freezing and thawing that came with early spring began to turn the war torn countryside into a frozen, rutty, muddy mess, the 23rd Infantry drove forward step by step; slow, tough, and steady with the cannon of two different tank companies crying out death threats to the enemy in support of the advance.

The next day found Chet Thiessen and his unit being slammed by a Chinese artillery barrage. Though the Army would not recognize his sacrifice until nearly twenty-seven months later, Corporal Thiessen was awarded the Purple Heart for wounds received in combat this day.

Unwanted camouflage

"The Chinese were very good with their artillery, especially their mortars. One day our unit was severely pinned down in the open during a hell of a barrage. There was no cover where we were at so we just hugged the ground and held on. We were getting hammered pretty good, and there were some mud huts several yards away. Roy got the idea that there might be some cover near those huts. He wanted us to run over there, but Bernie and I decided to take our chances where we were because we didn't want to expose ourselves. There were shells falling everywhere and Roy lit out for those mud huts. He just made it to the first of them and a shell exploded close to him so he dove for cover and disappeared out of site. When the barrage was over, Roy came staggering back over to us covered with the most awful stuff and he smelled to high heaven.

Most Korean houses like the ones he ran to had a big covered hole outside the house where all the septic waste ran into. There were people who went around every day with a wagon and would clean these pits out with a scoop on the end of a long stick. When Roy dove for cover, he ended up landing in one of these 'honey holes' as we called them! He was a mess, and there were no showers for us for a long time. We razzed him for days and made him keep his distance. If we all didn't have a few chances to laugh from time to time I think we would have all gone insane."

Home on the horizon

On March 11, our heroes of Baker Company received remarkable news. The 2nd Division was forming plans for a rotation program for its soldiers. Morale ran high amongst the troops with hopes of home on the horizon for many of them. There would be many more months of fighting ahead for Chet Thiessen and his squad, many more ridges to climb and conquer, and a lot more death and destruction for both sides.

Chet Thiessen and Bernie Cartee had been together since Basic Training at Camp Funstun. They had been through the thick of the worst of the war together, but the time had finally come to part company.

"Bernie had been sent back to the aid station for medical treatment when he was wounded. We hadn't seen him for a few days. Roy and I and the rest of the guys were on the line as usual, and we could hear a jeep pull up down the way. I heard somebody yelling my name down the line. I thought 'Whoever that is better shut-up because they are going to give my position away!' But the guy kept calling out, 'Chet . . . Chet Thiessen!' Finally somebody pointed the guy in my direction. We saw this fellow walking up, and didn't recognize him because he was wearing Master Sergeant stripes on his jacket. But to our surprise it was Bernie Cartee!

He came up and jumped in the foxhole with us. We were happy to see he was o.k. because we had been worried something happened to him. I said, 'Bernie, you better give that guy back his jacket, if they catch you with those Master Sergeant stripes on they'll court-martial your behind!' Bernie told us it was his jacket and they were his stripes! Apparently when he was at the aid station in the rear area he was put on detail in the Officer's Mess. To

Bernie's good fortune they found out he was a heck of a cook, so they promoted him so he could be in charge of the Officer's Mess. Bernie went from a Private First Class to a Master Sergeant in less than a week, got his own jeep, and was now off the front line and running a warm mess outfit in the rear! I couldn't believe it."

Heading for home

As fall came, so did welcome news. As he was sitting in his foxhole manning his machine gun waiting for the word to move forward, Chet Thiessen was to get different orders. A sergeant crawled carefully up to his foxhole and whispered his name.

"Thiessen, your times up. You're goin' home. Turn that .30 over to somebody and report to the Command bunker."

In justifiable shock, it took a minute for him to realize what he had just been told. The Division rotation program was now in effect, and his adventure in the bloody soil of the Korean peninsula was finally over. After a stop for a time in Japan, he would be heading for home.

"I don't think I've ever been that shocked in my life. After a time, you just come to grips with the fact you are already dead. It's a strange mindset, but at least after a while you don't have to worry about the thought of dying. I had given up on ever going home, assuming at one point or another I would buy it like thousands of others I saw.

So when this guy came and told me, I almost slugged him because the first thing I thought of was who would have guts to play that cruel of a joke on anyone."

The memories of the last perilous months of savage combat in the frozen mountains and valleys of the Korean peninsula flashed back through his mind. He said quick good-byes to Roy Anderson and his other buddies nearby, finally giving up his trusted machine gun to Roy. Feeling somewhat uneasy and exposed with only his .45 pistol at his side, the young warrior eased himself out of the foxhole into a low crawl back to where he could safely stand up and stealthily made his way to the command bunker, and on his way home.

EPILOGUE:

LIFE GOES ON FOR THE WARRIOR

After his Korean combat tour was over, Corporal Chet Thiessen received orders to report to Camp Custer in Augusta, Michigan, just south of his home town of Grand Rapids and just outside of Battle Creek, the famed home of the Kellogg and

Post cereal companies. Camp Custer at one time was claimed to be one of the largest military bases in the world. The post was in its heyday during WWI, and hundreds of the old, two story wood barracks still spread far and wide as far as one could see.

Chet was assigned a little different duty after his year of combat, this time as the driver for the base commander. While in Korea, there was nowhere to spend any money, so he had sent most of his pay home to help support his mother back in the States. With the rest, he picked up a 49 Chevy. Barely able to get by on the meager Army paycheck, when he was off duty, he went into Battle Creek to see about picking up a part time job to make a little extra money.

A fateful encounter

On one of his job searching jaunts into town, he rolled into a small root beer stand called the Snow Cap. The Snow Cap was co-owned by two brothers, Gaylord and Wendell Wemple. The three hit if off right away, and Chet soon learned that both Gaylord and Wendell were WWII Army vets, and he was hired on the spot. The brothers took an immediate liking to the young soldier, even to the point of going right to the cash register and handing him some money in advance to take care of an immediate need. The next day Chet found himself at the grill of the Snow Cap, and at the beginning of a friendship with the two brothers that would last a lifetime.

His new job at the root beer stand would end up having more benefits than he could ever have hoped for. He didn't know yet about the beautiful young car hop Donna, Gaylord and Wendell's little sister.

Surprise in the Mess Hall

One day while waiting for the General to get out of a meeting so he could drive him back to his office, Chet took advantage of the time and slipped into one of the Camp Custer mess halls. As he passed through the line, he couldn't believe what he was seeing, and almost dropped his tray. There behind the counter running the crew was none other than his old buddy "Bayonetin' Bernie" Cartee!

When Chet called out in surprise to Bernie he had almost the same reaction. The sheer coincidence of the two of them going through basic training, airborne school, Korea, and now being stationed here at Camp Custer together was uncanny. The two shared a happy reunion, and ended up spending a lot of time together in the weeks that followed.

"After a while, I noticed a change in Bernie. We were both very different after the war, there was no doubt about that, but he became more distant. I could tell he wasn't happy, and later Bernie requested to go back to the war. I lost track of him after that."

Unwanted Exile

Donna Wemple began taking up all of Chet's free time, and as the days and weeks passed, the two began to see a possible future together unfolding. But the life of a soldier is often not his own, and Chet got some bad news handed him one day.

"I only had six months left in my enlistment, and I got orders to ship out to Germany!"

Frustrated, but obedient, Chet Thiessen,

Chet Thiessen with German friend Witt

reported for his new duty station, the Base Post Office unit in Headernheim, Germany. It was easy duty, mostly driving a delivery truck, but his heart ached to be back with Donna. It was intense time of learning and growing with her, and of resolving a critical issue in their relationship - that of religion. Donna was a devout Catholic, and Chet, devout at avoiding anything to do with religion.

When Chet was a boy, his family was active in their church, and often attended the old fashioned tent revivals that came to town. One night, when he was 12 years old, while attending one of these revivals with his mother and a friend, he and the friend decided to sneak out and get some air. When they did, they made a shocking discovery. The revival event boasted many faith healings would take place this evening, and everyone waited in excited anticipation for this to happen. As the boys poked around looking for something to do, they happened to see an ambulance pull up to the revival tent. The back doors opened and several men and women jumped out. A few others that were standing nearby handed the able bodied folks crutches, cane's, and even a wheelchair that the alleged crippled person walked over to and got in, and all were carefully led, suddenly limping, lame, and blind, into the crowded revival tent. All were "healed" of their phony physical ailments that evening. That and a few other events had caused Chet to view anything religious with suspicion. But God seemed to have other plans.

An unlikely friendship

One particular memory of a counter example to Chet's perceived insincerity of religion stuck with him was that of a military chaplain he happened to encounter during his airborne training with the 101st Airborne. He had never forgotten the old Catholic priest who jumped one day along with all the young trainees.

"This old priest, and I mean significantly older than us guys who were all teenagers, had jumped with us this day. We were all whipped from the jump and all the

training and were sitting and resting. But this old guy, who was obviously far more tired than all of us kept walking around from man to man and talking to the guys, seeing if there was anything they needed. I never forgot that. He didn't stand to gain anything from us, and appeared to be truly concerned for the needs of each person. I never forgot that example."

Little did Chet Thiessen know that when he got to Germany, many of his faith questions would not only come forward, but would also be answered. When he first met his roommate at the billeting for the Base Post Office, he didn't know what to think. Charlie Kehoe, a year older, and hailing from New York city, had left his studies for the Catholic Priesthood to join the Army in an effort to help support his mother and nearly a dozen siblings. Kehoe being a Fordham University scholar, two more opposite personalities could seemingly not have been found.

Reverend Charles Kehoe
Germany 1953

"When I first met Charlie, he was polishing his brass and spit shining his shoes. He was all grooming and crisp uniform and I was not. I

wasn't really sure how this was going to work out. We ended up hitting it off right away. He became my best friend, and has been so ever since. We've never lost touch."

This unlikely friendship would lead to Chet's fears of faith being quelled. After leaving the service Charles Kehoe would later return to the Seminary and become a Catholic Priest for the Brooklyn Diocese.

A new life for the warrior

As the weeks passed as well as many letters between Chet and Donna, one day a letter arrived in Donna's mailbox she didn't expect. It was from Charlie Kehoe. The letter said, "Set a date, it's really time you and Chet got married!"

After his enlistment was up, Chet headed back to Battle Creek, Michigan. Looking forward to a life with his sweetheart, in time he started a masonry contracting business and though he privately suffered the rest of his life from the effects of several combat related injuries, especially those from his time as a prisoner of war, became a well-known and successful stone masonry contractor. On February 23rd, 1957, Chet and Donna were married at the altar at St. Philip Catholic Church in Battle Creek, Michigan, and later would have six daughters and a son.

A private war

Chet tried to leave Korea behind and look forward to his new life and growing family that he devoted himself completely to. But he carried a secret suffering with him that he never even shared with the wife who was his best friend. He had battle scars on the outside that told one story, but other battle scars on the inside that told another. Even years after returning home and distracting himself with the cares of life, the abuse suffered while a prisoner of war and other combat related wounds continued to plague him.

He never talked about the war to his family and rarely anyone else for nearly 30 years until finally beginning to share bits and pieces of his war memories with his son. Then one day in a chance conversation with his son-in-law while taking a break from cutting firewood with him in the woods at the back of his small farm, Chet mentioned the Medal of Honor he was promised at Chipyong-ni for the first time. A few weeks later came the revelation that he had been a Prisoner of War.

A new kind of "mission" on the horizon

The revelation seemed to bring an obvious sense of relief to Chet, whose natural toughness and intensity made the change visibly evident over time. The catharsis or release that the sharing of his war memories provided also brought with it unexpected consequences; a virtual opening of a Pandora's Box flood of war memories and emotions that had been forcefully locked away for decades, caused suffering anew in the years that followed. Chet, now a new Grandfather, turned to God and his now fervent religious beliefs for solace, and though the war would never quite go away, God was not silent, and would soon lead Chet on a path that would help to change his life and in some way, the life of thousands of other warriors like him.

Of all the memories a combat veteran would have, there was one that continued to haunt him. That of the Catholic Chaplain he had witnessed during his airborne training. The wisdom of age had caused him to wonder about the example of this humble man to the young troops. The wisdom of age also had given him a different perspective on the reality of his mortality than he had as a combat soldier in the natural fearlessness of youth.

Through a unique opportunity offered through a missionary outreach program of his Catholic Diocese, Chet entered into a two year training program for lay ministry outreach. When he was finished he was asked what parish ministry program he was interested in working in. Some sought to visit the sick, some those that were shut-ins, some to aid migrant workers, others to teach catechism classes, but Chet's was not what anyone would have expected. He wanted to take his faith and experiences to the active duty and reserve forces training at his former military base, now known as Fort Custer Military Training Center, in Augusta, Michigan, a busy but now much smaller version of where he was stationed after rotating out of Korea in 1951.

"When I think about how close I came to death every day during the war, and where my life has led me, from the streets of Grand Rapids, to the battlefields of Korea, to husband, father, grandfather, and now, great-grandfather, I look back on these things and really shake my head in disbelief. I often wonder why I am alive; why I survived the war when so many that literally stood right beside me didn't. I also think about when I was young how I grew to resent both the Army, and religion with a passion. For a long time I think I resented just about everyone and everything - with a passion. Then one day I came face to face with God, and in time he actually sent me back to the Army, with religion! Life is full of surprises."

After a long and arduous journey, this unsuspecting warrior had come full circle.

TESTIMONY TO A WARRIOR

Though now 81 years old, for nearly 30 years Chet Thiessen has donated, and continues to donate, without any compensation, every weekend to the thousands of troops training annually at Fort Custer Military Training Center in Augusta, Michigan as a lay chaplain representing the Catholic Diocese of Kalamazoo. Due to the shortage of military chaplains, he is often the only Catholic representative seeing to the particular needs of over 1100 Catholic soldiers in the Michigan National Guard. His service has also taken him to local Marine Corps and Naval Reserve centers, and Fort Custer National Cemetery. In cooperation with the Department of Military Affairs and the Diocese of Kalamazoo, he currently works alongside other military chaplains administering Catholic, Protestant, and Jewish religious services.

The wisdom of life and combat seen through the eyes of this warrior, as shared in individual and group talks, has helped many of our young troops returning from Iraq and Afghanistan who struggle with their own combat memories and adjustment to daily life.

The Adjutant General of Michigan has awarded Chet Thiessen the Distinguished Service Medal and two Legion of Merit medals in recognition of his dedicated service.

APPENDIX:
A QUEST FOR THE MEDAL OF HONOR

When Chet finally revealed to his family that he had been recommended for the Medal of Honor in Korea but never received it, a fledgling effort was established to find out why, and to see if there was any way he could still be awarded it.

Chet learned from his military contacts that a time waiver may be required of the Army regulation that required the recommendation to be made within two years of the event, and that eye witness testimony was imperative. Supporters of the effort came from all quarters. A retired police officer was able to quickly locate Chet's old Army buddies Bernard Cartee and Roy Anderson. Bernie lived in Iowa and Roy in northern Michigan. While a retired Judge who was a longtime family friend drafted sworn affidavits to be signed by the eye witnesses, Chet made an anxious phone call to Bernie. The author of this book happened to be present when the phone call was made. The emotional encounter was touching.

"Bernie, this is Chet." He said in halting voice.

"Chet! I don't believe it!" The surprised and happy voice at the other end of the phone could be heard. Suddenly there was silence, and a long pause as both men broke down into tears for reasons that only the two of them could have understood. After a few moments, the two "tough" combat vets were able to compose themselves. After an exchange where the two asked how each other had been doing, the reason for the call came up.

"Bernie, the reason I'm calling is -"

"Chet, I know why your calling. What took you so long?" Everyone present could hear said back. "I still remember when you lost that blue handled knife you liked so much."

After a heartfelt reunion by phone, Chet and Donna went to Iowa to meet with Bernie, who gladly signed the affidavit testifying to the deeds of Corporal Chet Thiessen at Chipyong-ni, Korea, and the witnessed promise of the Medal of Honor by the officers in charge that day. Soon, the couple travelled to northern Michigan to meet with Roy Anderson who also gladly signed an affidavit of eye-witness.

A Bill was introduced in 1986 by U.S. Congressman Howard Wolpe to effect the legislation thought necessary to approve the time waiver. The Bill went dead at the end of the congressional session, and Mr. Wolpe was not re-elected. Years went by with Chet Thiessen under the impression that the Bill was still in committee being evaluated. He wrote letter after letter to anyone he could think of, including two Presidents, only to receive generic "sorry but . . ." letters each time.

In 1994 a family member got involved to see if they could get the ball rolling again. Other supportive affidavits came in from retired LTC Emil Stryker, formerly 23rd Infantry Able Company Executive Officer, and a letter from retired four-star General Paul Freeman, formerly the 23rd Infantry Commander, both present at the battle of Chipyong-ni. All evidence and supportive documentation available at the time, including dozens of letters of support from civil and military leaders, as well as private citizens, was compiled into a booklet that was sent to every Congressman and Senator in Washington, D.C. serving on military affairs committees asking for help and consideration. The effort took months and the last of the family's limited means, and was basically ignored. It seemed Korea was not only the "forgotten war" but a war that everyone still wanted to forget, to include forgetting about the veterans that fought it as well.

Finally, in 1997, U.S. Congressman Nick Smith stepped into the void and both introduced new legislation to have the time limitations waived, and forwarded the matter to the Military Awards Branch for Chet Thiessen to finally be considered for the Medal of Honor he was recommended for on that frozen Korean battlefield decades before. An awards committee was established to review the information available, but the result was not in Chet's favor. Apparently, though they did not disclose the reason why in their response, later it was learned there were other technicalities in military regulations regarding the award of the Medal of Honor they claimed prohibited them awarding it to Chet.

In 2013, and appeal effort was initiated, based on new evidence. Thanks much to Chet's former Baker Company commander, now retired LTC Sherman Pratt, then Judge Advocate for the Korean War Veterans Association, who sent Chet a copy of a book he authored, *Decisive Battles of the Korean War* published by Vantage Press, New York (1992), other corroborative evidence was gathered, along with a second affidavit by Bernard Cartee. A comprehensive case was compiled by the author of this book and then introduced by U.S. Congressman Justin Amash. This time he went straight to the top, directly to Secretary of the Army John McHugh, who pledged to give the matter full consideration.

Weeks later, the news arrived. The new evidence was not enough to trump the Army regulations that were blocking the award. Apparently, according to officials at the Army Awards Branch, without the original recommendation form dated from Chet's time in Korea, signed by two levels of command, even if the

Army favored the award, regulation bound them from being able to award it. Hoping to find a way to still honor Chet's valor, Army officials suggested a new request for an alternative medal for valor that they would be free to consider be submitted.

It was a difficult decision for Chet Thiessen to make. He wasn't out to just get a medal. He had lots of them, and at 81, the recognition it would bring seemed somewhat insignificant. His 27 year quest for the Medal of Honor was not so much about getting a medal as it was about closure of something deeply personal he could never explain in words. Finally, at the request of his family, friends, military acquaintances, and a whole host of other supporters who pleaded with Chet to allow the matter to be considered, finally consented. A new submission is pending.

###

Thank you for reading *Through the Eyes of the Warrior*. It has been a pleasure to share these memories of an American war hero, and give testimony to all of the intrepid American soldiers that fought the Korean War. **- Tim Schoonard**

HISTORICAL REFERENCES:

• Headquarters 23rd RCT, *After Action Report* Covering Operations of the 23rd Regimental Combat Team During the Period 130011 to 1524001 Feb 51, 3 March 1951

• Headquarters 23rd RCT, *After Action Report* Covering Operations of the 23rd Regimental Combat Team During the Period 290630 Jan to 152400 Feb 51., 13 March 1951

• Headquarters, 23rd Infantry Regiment, Secret *Command Report*: 1 November 1950 thru 30 November 1950 (Declassified 27 December 1997) http://www.koreanwar.org

• Headquarters, 23rd Infantry Regiment, Secret *Command Report*: 1 December 1950 thru 31 December 1950 (Declassified 27 December 1997) http://www.koreanwar.org

• Headquarters, 23rd Infantry Regiment, Secret *Command Report*: 1 January 1951 thru 31 January 1951 (Declassified 25 January 1997) http://www.koreanwar.org

• Headquarters, 23rd Infantry Regiment, Secret *Command Report*: 1 February 1951 thru 28 February 1951 (Declassified 19 September 1998) http://www.koreanwar.org

• Headquarters, 23rd Infantry Regiment, Secret *Command Report*: 1 March 1951 thru 31 March 1951 (Declassified 25 January 1997) http://www.koreanwar.org

• Joseph, St., Seminary and College, *The Catholic Encyclopedia*, McGraw-Hill, 1965.

•Monroe, Clark C., Lieutenant, *Second to None: The Second United States Infantry Division in Korea 1950-1951*, Toppan Printing Co., Tokyo, Japan (according to the text, this non-copyrighted work compiled by 2nd Infantry Division historians at Kapyong, Korea, 15 November 1951)

•Pratt, Sherman W., LTC, U.S. Army, Retired, *Decisive Battles of the Korean War*, Vantage Press, New York, 1992.

ACKNOWLEDGEMENTS:

I want to thank all the many people who made this book possible. First, my beloved wife who has infinite patience with my insatiable desire to write, and has been a wellspring of encouragement for me to keep moving forward with it. Thanks to all my seven kids, who at one point or another have lent tech or other support to dear old Dad to help me get my books done.

To Chet and Donna Thiessen for the many hours of interviews, phone calls, and photo hunts that allowed me to compile this amazing story of someone who was both a war, and post-war hero, and to my highly trained and competent daughter Monica for technical editing support.

I would also like to thank the folks at the Korean War Project for making war records conveniently available to everyone, and the Director of the 2nd Infantry Division museum in Korea, for his input and advice.

About the Author:

Tim Schoonard is a professional furniture artisan, U.S. Army veteran, and the author of two other books, *Wolves in Sheep's Clothing* and *Taking Part in the Work*, as well as several articles. He writes from his studio in southwest Michigan.

www.timschoonard.com

CPSIA information can be obtained
at www.ICGtesting.com
Printed in the USA
BVHW04s0153171018
530410BV00021B/560/P